F IN MOUTH

FAMOUS IRISH POLITICAL GAFFES

Shane Coleman

Cartoons by Fintan Taite

MENTOR
BOOKS

First Published in 2006 by

MENTOR BOOKS
43 Furze Road
Sandyford Industrial Estate
Dublin 18
Republic of Ireland

Tel: + 353 1 295 2112 / 3   Fax: + 353 1 295 2114
e-mail: admin@mentorbooks.ie
www.mentorbooks.ie

ISBN-10: 1-84210-376-8
ISBN-13: 978-1-84210-376-0

A catalogue record for this book
is available from the British Library

Editor: Treasa O'Mahony
Typesetting: Artwerk Ltd
Book Design : Nicola Sedgwick
Cover Design: Anú Design
Cover Image & Text Illustrations: Fintan Taite www.fintantaite.com

Printed in Ireland by ColourBooks Ltd.
1 3 5 7 9 10 8 6 4 2

Foreword

The idea of *Foot In Mouth* is to recount in one collected work the major gaffes committed by politicians since the foundation of this State. Some gaffes are funny - with little impact other than a passing embarrassment for the 'gaffer'. Others are deadly serious – in some cases, effectively ending political careers. Nobody likes to be reminded of their mistakes, but politicians are exposed to public scrutiny in a way in which few others will ever experience. Therefore, it is an unfortunate, but inevitable, hazard of their occupation that any gaffes they make will quickly become public record.

It is no accident that the people who feature most often in this book are those who reached the very top of Irish politics. They have made countless important decisions throughout their careers, so it is not surprising that sometimes they got it wrong. The gaffes or errors detailed in *Foot In Mouth* are no reflection of the capability or talent of those who made them.

I would like to thank my family and friends and most particularly Ev, Cúan and Donagh for all their support. A special thanks to Danny McCarthy at Mentor Books, who came up with the original idea for this book. Thanks also to Treasa O'Mahony at Mentor for all her help, guidance and patience. Special thanks to Stephen, Martin, Mick and Paul for their invaluable advice and to all my colleagues at the *Sunday Tribune*. I would also like to thank the staff at the National Library for their unfailing courtesy and cooperation.

Shane Coleman

September 2006

For permission to reproduce copyright material, the publishers would like to thank the following:

- Blackwater Press for *One Spin on the Merry-Go-Round* by Sean Duignan; *Jack Lynch, a Biography* by TP O'Mahony
- The Mercier Press for *Short Fellow: A Biography of Charles J Haughey* by Ryle T Dwyer
- Brandon/MountEagle Publications for *The Road from Ardoynne: The Making of a President* by Ray Mac Manais
- Gill & Macmillan for *Breaking the Mould: How the PDs changed Irish Politics* by Stephen Collins; *All in a Life: An Autobiography by Garret Fitzgerald*; *Hiding Behind a Face: Fine Gael Under Fitzgerald* by Stephen O'Byrnes
- Poolbeg Press for *The Boss: Charles J Haughey in Government* by Joe Joyce and Peter Murtagh
- Aherlow Press for *Charles J Haughey, the Survivor* by Raymond Smith; *Garret the Enigma* by Raymond Smith
- Hodder & Staughton for *Mary Robinson: An Authorised Biography* by Olivia O'Leary and Helen Burke
- Cambridge University Press for *Ireland, 1912–1985: Politics and Society* by Joe Lee
- Dublin and London 1970 for *Eamon De Valera* by Lord Longford
- The O'Brien Press for *The Haughey File* by Stephen Collins
- London, HarperCollins for *Haughey, His Life and Unlucky Deeds* by Bruce Arnold
- New Island Books for *Snakes & Ladders* by Fergus Finlay
- Cambridge University Press for *Ireland, 1912–1985: Politics & Society* by Joe Lee
- *Hot Press* magazine for extracts from John Waters' interview with Charles Haughey (1984)

Contents

Black is the Colour

Mary O'Rourke

THE BACKGROUND

In January 2006, Seanad leader and former government minister Mary O'Rourke had just won a tightly-fought convention vote. She had been selected as a Fianna Fáil candidate for Longford-Westmeath for the next general election.

THE GAFFE

Speaking after the result was announced, O'Rourke paid tribute to her team: 'They listened to my moaning and groaning . . . they were there for me and they worked like blacks'.

THE IMPACT

The comment, according to the next day's newspapers, led to a wave of murmurs, apparently of disapproval, among the delegates. Murmurs of disapproval would be heard for a few days to come.

A number of anti-racism groups described the comment as inappropriate and ill-judged.

However, in interviews in the ensuing days, a largely unrepentant O'Rourke said she meant no offence, telling RTÉ radio: 'It was meant in a complimentary fashion, praising the hard work of my team and indirectly myself . . . There was absolutely no offence meant. It is a well-known phrase in Ireland, but perhaps in a different Ireland, it's no longer relevant. Perhaps I should say "like Trojans" but then would you be upsetting the Greeks or something, I don't know'.

She claimed the furore was 'political correctness gone wrong'.

The controversy died down within days, as people accepted O'Rourke was in no way racist. Peter O'Mahony, chief executive of the Irish Refugee Council, said that while the comment was 'clearly ill-advised', O'Rourke was one of the relatively small number of national politicians who had been brave and courageous on refugee issues.

Fellow senator and Fine Gael TD Paul Coghlan also came to O'Rourke's defence, stating: 'It was a saying in our youth. It was meant in a non-harmful way'.

A few weeks later, at a meeting of the Fianna Fáil parliamentary party, TDs and senators exploded into laughter when a speaker, addressing the meeting after a rousing contribution from Senator Mary White, told them that they would have to 'work like Whites' in the run-up to the general election.

The F**king Peace Process

John Bruton

THE BACKGROUND

John Bruton fulfilled his ambition of becoming Taoiseach at the end of 1994. The Fianna Fáil/Labour government collapsed and Fine Gael joined forces with Labour and the Democratic Left to form a 'Rainbow Coalition' with Bruton at the helm. As Albert Reynolds, his predecessor in the job, had discovered Northern Ireland and the evolving, highly complex peace process would take up a huge amount of the Taoiseach's time.

THE GAFFE

In April 1995, Bruton was in Cork attending a Fine Gael fundraising lunch at the Imperial Hotel. He agreed to do an interview with a reporter from the local radio station 96FM. According to reports, the Taoiseach acted in an agitated manner throughout the interview, before ordering the reporter to turn off

her recorder. When she complied, Bruton was reported to have said: 'I am sick of answering questions about the f**king peace process'. A Fine Gael activist reportedly suggested to the reporter that she ask about water charges. The reporter refused and left after the Taoiseach made a half-hearted apology. Within days, details of the Taoiseach's angry tirade had reached the national media.

THE IMPACT

The reporter told a Sunday newspaper that the incident had 'stunned' her. 'The language he used was the last thing I would expect from a Taoiseach, especially considering the sensitivity of that subject. I was extremely angry. Maybe the man was tired, but what he said was not something you should say to anybody.'

A spokesman for Bruton responded that the Taoiseach had 'no quarrel' with the reporter, who was just doing her job and who he 'regarded highly'. Bruton himself said he could understand 'her being upset because I was very upset myself at finding myself in a situation I did not want to be in. I thought I was being interviewed on local issues and I was not prepared for an interview on that subject. I expressed my frustration quite strongly. I can't honestly say whether I used bad language or not. I was in a stressed state, but if I caused offence I am very sorry'.

The incident was largely defused when Bruton faxed a letter of apology to the offices of 96FM. The station's news editor told the *Cork Examiner*: 'We are happy to accept the Taoiseach's apology and to leave it at that'.

The incident, though often recalled, did not do any lasting damage to the Taoiseach, although it was seen as embarrassing due to the sensitivity of the subject matter. There is little doubt also that in the 1997 general election, Bertie Ahern was seen as being stronger on Northern Ireland than Bruton – an important factor in what was a very tight election. Although the nation cringed at the Taoiseach using such unparliamentary language, at some level it understood what he meant by the comment. Bruton, though, was less than six months in the job when he made that outburst. Imagine how Bertie Ahern must feel after a decade dealing with the 'f**king peace process'.

3

BSE in the VIP

Ivan Yates

THE BACKGROUND

It was October 1996 and the Russians were coming – or at least the Russian Agriculture Ministry's veterinary service. They were meeting with Russia's permanent veterinary official in Ireland to discuss the future of the beef trade between the two countries in light of the incidence of BSE in Irish cows. Only a tiny number of Irish cows had been infected, but the level of the problem in Britain had caused unease in foreign markets and the Russians wanted to ensure that the beef their country was receiving was BSE-free.

During the week-long visit, there was ongoing and intense discussions between the Russian and Irish officials. Both the Agriculture Minister Ivan Yates and the Taoiseach John Bruton hosted dinners for the Russians. However, by the Friday, the Russians were proposing that a ban should be imposed on the export of beef from seven counties – Wexford, Longford, Donegal, Limerick, Cork, Tipperary and Monaghan. Yates, after talking to the Taoiseach, instructed his officials not to accept the plan.

The following morning, as the Russian officials prepared to leave, Irish officials went to Dublin Airport to meet them and a last minute compromise was thrashed out in the VIP lounge. Yates was not present – he was conducting a constituency clinic in Kavanagh's Pub in Enniscorthy – but was in constant phone contact with his officials. A protocol was signed prohibiting the sale of beef to Russia from three counties: Tipperary, Cork and Monaghan.

It was as good a deal as any that could have been achieved in the circumstances. At one point Ireland had been facing a total ban from 1 November so some compromise from the Irish government was inevitable. That didn't stop the Irish Farmers' Association from venting its anger and, naturally, the three counties affected were not pleased with the decision.

THE GAFFE

The following weekend, Yates went on RTÉ's *The Week in Politics* programme and during a discussion about the controversial protocol, the Minister argued that the deal had been done under serious pressure – a gun had been put to his head. He used the words: 'I did a deal with the Russians last Saturday at 1pm in the VIP lounge at Dublin Airport'.

THE IMPACT

The main opposition parties, Fianna Fáil and the PDs, were quick to pounce in the Dáil in the days after his appearance on

The Week in Politics. In response to a Dáil question from Des O'Malley, Yates had to confirm that he was not present at the airport when the deal was signed. A spokesman for Yates explained that the comment on RTÉ was made 'in the heat of the moment' and the Minister had intended to say he had 'authorised the deal in Dublin Airport through his officials'. But the clarification did nothing to assuage Fianna Fáil and the PDs. It was suddenly open season on Yates. O'Malley said that Yates had 'some neck' to suggest there was a gun to his head, sarcastically stating that the 'Russians must have been using one of their intercontinental ballistic missiles'. There were acrimonious scenes in the Dáil with heated demands from the opposition for Yates to apologise for giving the impression that he was in the airport when the deal was done.

Fianna Fáil leader Bertie Ahern asked the Taoiseach if it was acceptable that a Minister should mislead the public by creating the false impression that a gun was put to his head; that he was there to the final stages; 'that he actually got the dust of the Russian veterinary officers' boot into the face'. He went on: 'The Minister offered to travel to Moscow but apparently he did not travel up the road to Dublin Airport . . . The gun that was held to his head must have been one of those long-range Iraqi super-guns'.

Going just a bit over the top, Ahern added: 'We were all given the impression that the Minister was some latter-day Michael Collins, facing from a Russian minister a threat of immediate and terrible war on the trade front, if he did not agree immediately to Russian demands. Why did he allow eleven days before correcting the record? In 1921, we had to sign away six counties. This time, we signed away another three. But the ultimatum did not even come from a Russian minister. It came from three vets. This is no sort of way of carrying on inter-government business'.

PD leader Mary Harney said Yates had misled the Dáil the previous day when he insisted he had never said he had been in Dublin Airport. Fianna Fáil's Noel Davern widened out the debate, asking why those particular three counties were chosen when Wexford – Yates' home constituency – had a higher incidence of BSE per capita than Tipperary or Cork. Brian Cowen turned the guns towards the bigger target of the Taoiseach. The extent of his involvement, Fianna Fáil's agriculture spokesman said, 'was in having a meal with the [Russian] delegation, which shows the sort of priority the matter received from the top down'. Yates responded that from his experience, 'some of the most important exchanges of views have taken place over a meal and a bottle of wine . . . I think it is part of the Irish charm offensive that we do that kind of thing rather well, if I may say so, particularly in the Department of Agriculture'.

In a prepared statement, he accepted that on *The Week in Politics* he said that he had done a deal with the Russians in the airport. 'It was one of many comments and many interviews. It was a sentence out of what had been a two day debate on the matter. However, if I created a misleading impression then I apologise for that. I regret also that in a comment in the House yesterday, I may have unwittingly misled deputies on this subject. I simply had forgotten that I used that sentence. What I meant was that I effected the deal, agreed to it, and took full responsibility for it,' Yates said. He also said that the Taoiseach knew all along that he was not at the airport. 'He was of the view that there was no need for me to be there.'

He was right of course. Officials always do the real negotiating and there is little doubt that Yates and the government had done everything they could and pulled off a pretty good deal in the circumstances. However, in terms of perception – which is everything in politics – the optics were all wrong. *The Irish Times* summed it up with a very prominent front-page cartoon. The caption said: 'Transparency in Government – example number 432. Minister Yates signs the Russian beef deal at the airport'. And it featured what was obviously a Russian official saying: 'Nice to not see you again Minister'.

Hot Press - Cool Charlie

Charlie Haughey

THE BACKGROUND

December 1984: Charlie Haughey was biding his time on the opposition benches. He had been out of power for two years. However, after miraculously surviving three leadership heaves in the early 1980s, he was in total control of his party for the first time. With the Fine Gael and Labour ruling coalition struggling to survive the worst economic conditions since the grim 1950s, it was only a matter of time before Haughey was Taoiseach once again.

THE GAFFE

That month, Haughey agreed to do an interview with *Hot Press* magazine. The journalist who did the interview was John Waters – who became one of the country's best known journalists – and what emerged was arguably the frankest, most revealing interview with 'The Boss' ever printed. It landed Haughey in a fair bit of hot water because of his use of profanities and his revelation that he always had a hidden desire to 'knock off BMWs'.

Over two decades on, it's still a great read. Waters began his piece by taking the reader through the different stages of the interview – including being vetted by Haughey himself at a sort of pre-interview. According to Waters, this was so Haughey could reassure himself that Waters wasn't going to come out with what PJ Mara 'eloquently summed up' as 'any of that Arms Trial shite'.

Waters wrote: 'P.J. is very good on the subject of what happens when people do. Or when they confront The Boss with Sean Doherty, telephone tapping and tape-recorders. "The shutters come down," says P.J., illustrating graphically with both hands the downward motion of imaginary shutters descending to obscure Charles J. Haughey's face. "The fuse starts to burn. And then you've had it".'

But instead of lighting the fuse, Waters skilfully draws out the interviewee and provides a fascinating insight into Haughey the man, as opposed to Haughey the politician that everyone had known for a quarter of a century at that stage.

It's clear from reading the early part of the piece that Haughey likes Waters and is willing to open up. During the pre-interview interview, Waters explained to Haughey that he would like to focus in particular on Haughey's own experiences as a young person. 'Sure I'd never be able to remember that far back! That's a long time ago'.

Prompted further by Haughey about the subject matter, Waters mentions crime and vandalism. Haughey's response is detailed as follows: ' "Well what could I say about that?"

he thinks out loud. "I don't think I could say that I approve of youngsters knocking off BMWs and so on," he muses. "Although, I must admit, I always had a hidden desire to do something like that! I don't suppose I could say anything like that, now could I?" '

Waters stressed that the whole point of the interview is to portray the lighter, more personal side of Charlie Haughey, which doesn't normally come across in the media. Most people see him as an austere individual.

' "Oh but I am austere," he responds, deadpan. "Deep down I'm very austere." There isn't the merest flicker of a smile. The reporter meets his stare, wondering if he's supposed to laugh. He does. So does Charles J. Haughey.' Waters has passed the audition and an interview date is arranged.

During that interview, Haughey talks about his passion for football and hurling in his younger days and being a teenager during 'The Emergency'. 'Literally, we only saw a policeman when he came to stop us playing football on the road! Of course we robbed orchards and things like that, but there was no great tension about it.'

Because there was no work, Haughey recalled that many of his peers either joined the Irish or British army. 'And kids, if they were in a rebellious mood, and were, y'know, rowing with their teachers or parents, they'd go 'Fuck you! I'll go off and join the British army if you don't appreciate me or treat me properly!'

Asked if he was aware of being different or special in any way as a young man, Haughey laughed and responded: 'Oh Jesus Christ, no!!'

Haughey also spoke about how his children 'treat me like a semi-imbecile, because I don't know how to work tape-recorders and videos, and record things! And, y'know, when I'm going out and there's a programme on television that I want to record on the video, I have to get one of them to do it. They say: "Ah, go away! Leave it to me. I'll do it for you!" '

Music comes up in conversation and Haughey speaks freely about the Beatles, dance halls, the Clancy Brothers, the Fureys, the Dubliners, the Chieftains and Boy George ('He seems a bit weird').

Haughey resisted playing to the gallery when asked if there should be a mechanism to allow young people to have quicker access to politics. 'Politics is not the Boy Scouts! It's a bit of a haul. And I think, per se, it has to be; you've to sort of win your spurs and fight your way through . . . Experience counts a lot in politics'.

Haughey also contended that 'everybody hates politicians!' not just young people. 'Old people are not any different. The ordinary guy in the pub thinks politicians are all useless and crooked and so on. That's not confined to young people. That's a healthy cynicism and distrust which most modern democracies – and certainly the Irish people – have always had, at all ages.'

He says that Irish people are 'tremendous politicians. They're fascinated with politics. The ordinary guy in the pub can talk more intelligently and more wisely and with more depth about politics than anybody in any country in the world. Certainly he's about fifty times ahead of his bovine English counterpart, who knows about Margaret Thatcher and maybe one or two others – but that's all he knows.'

In the most controversial and best remembered part of the interview, Haughey is asked about the aspect of Ireland or Irish society which angers him the most. At first he gives a fairly neutral answer about not being able to live anywhere else and not being perpetually angry about anything. Then Waters notes that 'he pauses at length and reflects, he looks me straight in the eye before continuing . . . "I could instance a load of fuckers whose throats I'd cut and push over the nearest cliffs, but there's no percentage in that!" (Laughs).'

Haughey opens up further: 'Smug people. I hate smug people. People who think they know it all. I know from my own experiences that nobody knows it all. Some of these commentators who purport to a smug knowallness, who pontificate . . . They'll say something today and they're totally wrong about it – completely wrong – and they're shown to be wrong about it. Then the next day they're back, pontificating the same as ever. That sort of smug, knowall commentator – I suppose if anything annoys me, that annoys me. But I don't have sleepless nights about it.'

On a lighter note, Haughey laments that 'to my dying day, I'll regret that I was too late for the free society! We missed out on that! It came too late for my generation!'

He goes on to add that 'when I was young . . . authority was much more of a thing. Authority in society, in the community, in school, and of course the guards. You were afraid of the guards. Nowadays, kids aren't: they just call them "pigs", y'know? But in my day, if a guard said to you "fuck off", you fucked off as quick as you could! There was far more authority, and that was a big change. Kids nowadays have developed their own ethos and mores. And I think we've changed as parents too. I think we were much more understanding and sympathetic to our children than our parents were to us. My mother knew what was best for me, and told me what to do, and what not to do, and insisted that I did or didn't do it. I wasn't like that with my children. We certainly trusted them far more. We felt that what you had to do was just give them a home where they knew they were important, where they were loved and where they were trusted and where they could always come back to. If they made a fuck-up of things, they could always come back home and they would be welcomed and looked after and protected and helped.'

Haughey also spoke about his love for his island of Inishvickillane and reading and his dislike of television. 'I think most television is tripe. Boring rubbish. To me, television is the news, or occasionally some very good documentary-type programmes. Very few. The News, some documentaries and sport.'

Asked if he ever saw *Dallas* – hugely popular at the time – he laughed and said: 'I see them because I have to confess that in my home there are those who look at *Dallas*. And well, I might go and do a bit of work, but sometimes I might sit through it. I really think it's shit. I think it's terrible shit. But then I know that's a minority view. (Laughs.) I think most people think it's shit, like, but they look at it all the same.'

He said his hero growing up was Sean Lemass, 'the greatest human being that I ever met. Or could ever hope to meet.' Asked about the greatest quality in a friend, he responded: 'Well, there was a great word, d'ya see, that Sean Lemass in his whole life instanced but could never pronounce. Like most Dublin people, he could never pronounce 'loyalty' – he always pronounced it 'loylaty'. And I think that's the most important thing: loyalty. A Dublin man's loylaty. Not loyalty, because that's something different. But loylaty. I think that's the most important characteristic in friends.'

Towards the end of the interview, Waters asks him if there was a day in his life that he remembers as the happiest? Haughey

responds: 'Oh, FUCK OFF!! (Laughs) No!!! You're turning into a fuckin' woman's diary columnist now!'

THE IMPACT

The interview is included as a gaffe because Haughey's use of bad language, particularly the line about the 'load of fuckers whose throats I'd cut and push over the nearest cliffs', caused a lot of controversy. There was criticism in some quarters that Haughey was simply using the language in an attempt to be cool and hip with young people but others question whether he thought the language would be edited out. The weekend after the interview was published, the *Sunday Press* quoted a 'close party aide' as saying that Haughey was 'a bit surprised' that his colourful language was included in the interview, adding: 'But he seems alright. But sure everybody effs and blinds a bit in conversation like that.' Whether it was intentional or not, it is highly doubtful as to whether it caused any damage to Haughey. The fact that the profanities were in print, rather than spoken on radio or TV certainly diminished their impact.

Albert Reynolds got into a lot more trouble for simply using the word 'crap' on television eight years later. And while some people would have been offended by the use of bad language, to others it may even have added to the whiff of sulphur that surrounded Haughey and perhaps even appealed to younger voters. Certainly, anybody reading the whole interview would have come away with a more positive impression of Haughey. Unfortunately, the outrage caused by his use of profanities overshadowed a lot of the genuinely interesting and innovative things Haughey proposed in the interview, such as his thoughts on encouraging creativity through schools. The main national newspapers naturally picked up on the interview and the use of bad language but wrote rather straight news pieces about it. Under the headine: 'Charlie Haughey hates smug know-alls', *The Irish Times* simply outlined the most interesting parts of the interview and included the word 'Fuckers' without the use of asterix. *The Irish Press* ran a lighter piece, headlined: 'Haughey lets his hair down', which said that 'the lighter and more personal side of Charles J Haughey reveals how he regrets missing out on the permissive society, had a hidden desire to steal a BMW and would like to cut the throats of some 'f......' in an extraordinary interview in this week's edition of *Hot Press*.'

The interview was a major coup for *Hot Press*, adding to its reputation as a magazine that got people to open up and say things they would not dream of saying to any other media outlet. Haughey, meanwhile, returned to power at the next general election in early 1987 and served for another five years as Taoiseach.

Presumed Guilty

Mary Harney

THE BACKGROUND

It was May 2000 and there was massive attention on the tribunals in Dublin Castle. There was a public outcry as it emerged at the Moriarty Tribunal that former Taoiseach Charlie Haughey had received over ten and a half million euro from business people over 17 years. Meanwhile, the Fianna Fáil/Progressive Democrats government of the day was having its own problems and was reeling over a massive backlash against its move to appoint former Judge Hugh O'Flaherty to the European Investment Bank. (See Chapter 24).

THE GAFFE

In an interview with the *Irish Independent* at the end of a tough week for the government, the Tanaiste, Mary Harney, said her old nemesis Haughey should be jailed for the way in which he used top political office to gather cash for himself. The *Independent* reported that 'without a moment's hesitation she made clear her view that the one-time FF leader should spend time in prison.' 'I do, yes,' she said. 'He should be convicted'. Dismissing the idea that Haughey should not go to jail because of his age, Harney declared: 'That doesn't wash with me, not when people have used public office for their own gain as he did'.

The problem was that Haughey was facing trial in the Circuit Criminal Court, charged with obstructing the McCracken Tribunal – the first tribunal to look into his affairs – between March and July 1997. Unsurprisingly, Haughey sought to stop the trial, alleging he couldn't get a fair trial because of such public comments.

THE IMPACT

The complaint was upheld by Judge Kevin Haugh who placed an indefinite stay on Haughey's trial, with Harney's comments cited as a major reason for the postponement. The judge found there was a 'real and substantial' risk that Haughey would not receive a fair trial because of Harney's claims that he should be jailed for a long time. He said he was satisfied that a jury could be influenced by comments, either consciously or subconsciously. He also said a march organised by various political groups against 'corrupt politicians' would further prejudice Haughey's right to a fair trial.

The judge maintained that Harney's comments were liable to influence jurors to such an extent that they would 'dilute or diminish' the presumption of innocence an accused person should enjoy. The risk of a juror being influenced by Ms Harney's comments was enhanced, he said, by her 'high standing and reputation for integrity', and her special or pre-eminent position to make assessments or to express informed views on the matters in question. Judge Haugh said he was satisfied that the Tanaiste was not speaking of the obstruction charges in the interview, but this did not detract from the gravity of Mr Haughey's complaint that she had prejudiced his right to a fair trial.

Harney found herself at the centre of a major political storm. Instead of getting praise for her tough line on Haughey, she was villified for helping get him off the hook from the most serious threat he faced. The charge carried with it a possible jail sentence on conviction, though a suspended sentence or fine was regarded as more likely. There were calls for her resignation in the Dáil.

Harney was said to be 'very cut up' by the ruling and actually offered her resignation to Taoiseach Bertie Ahern. Had it been accepted, it could have brought down the FF/PD coalition and led to a general election. However, Ahern refused to accept the resignation. On the same day, Harney raised the issue of her continuing leadership of the PDs with three or four senior colleagues, including former leader Des O'Malley and then Minister of State Liz O'Donnell. They were said to have strongly dissuaded her from resigning.

Haughey was reportedly delighted with developments, particularly because his old enemy, Harney, was to blame for his good fortune. According to one report, Haughey responded to a friend's comment that 'God looks after his own' by saying: 'He f**king took long enough'.

Despite the furore, the controversy soon died down and there was no long term damage to Harney. Two years later, her party was returned to government in a general election that saw the PDs double its seat numbers.

All Politics is Local
Willie O'Dea

THE BACKGROUND

The closing months of 2000 proved to be something of a winter of discontent for the taxi industry. Following a High Court ruling, the government moved to end the system of control over the number of taxi licences by deregulating the industry across the country. There was massive public support for the measure as it was blindingly obvious that there were not enough taxis on the roads. However, not everyone in Dáil Eireann was supportive of the measure. A number of government backbenchers and opposition TDs – concerned about how the decision would play in their constituencies – spoke out against the move.

THE GAFFE

Fianna Fáil TD Willie O'Dea, then a Junior Minister in the Department of Education, also came out against deregulation.

He had already said that deregulation was 'not the answer' to what was 'essentially [a] Dublin-based problem'. However, he was then recorded – unbeknownest to him – at an gathering of angry taxi drivers in Limerick saying that the decision to deregulate the industry was disastrous and would not work in practice. He urged the taxi drivers to 'keep the pressure on' for change. O'Dea also referred to the Minister of State for the Environment, Bobby Molloy, as impertinent and described his handling of the taxi issue as disastrous. To the added annoyance of the party leadership, O'Dea also spoke on local radio, expressing solidarity with the policy of deregulation with which he personally did not agree.

THE IMPACT

The comments were a major embarrassment for the government at a time when it needed to keep a united front against strong opposition from the taxi lobby. It was one thing for backbenchers to come out against government policy, but quite another for a Minister of State to do so.

The comments prompted Fine Gael to put down a motion in the Dáil calling for O'Dea's removal from office. Fine Gael's transport spokeswoman Olivia Mitchell said the Taoiseach should immediately sack Mr O'Dea for his 'disgraceful attempt to shirk collective Government responsibility'. The deputy's 'pathetic attempt to pander to the taxi lobby was further evidence of Fianna Fáil wanting to have it both ways'. She added that O'Dea had compounded his offence by declaring that he had not realised some of his comments were being recorded.

Mitchell later told the Dáil debate on the motion that the Taoiseach's failure to fire O'Dea 'suggests to me and to many others that he agrees with Deputy O'Dea's view that the Government's decision was, to quote Deputy O'Dea, 'disastrous and unworkable', that 'there were impertinent people in government' who had been known to change their minds before, and that all that was required now was to keep up the pressure'.

O'Dea's reported remarks infuriated Tanaiste Mary Harney – who regarded them as the height of insolence – and did not impress Taoiseach Bertie Ahern. Harney publicly criticised O'Dea's attitude on the matter, stressing there would be no change in government policy and adding that any member of the government and any politician who advised taxi drivers or others that there would be change was being very foolish and was misleading the public.

Asked if O'Dea should be dismissed, Harney told RTÉ radio: 'Normally if somebody has such a fundamental disagreement with government policy, and this is an important area, then maybe they might consider their options themselves. Minister O'Dea doesn't intend to do that.'

Speaking in the Dáil, the Taoiseach said he could not stop people having certain views, but added bluntly that if these were contrary to the collective responsibility of the government he would not tolerate them. It also emerged that the government chief whip, Seamus Brennan – at the behest of the Taoiseach – spoke to O'Dea twice about his remarks. *The Sunday Business Post* reported at the time: 'On the first occasion, immediately in the wake of the revelations, Brennan formally warned O'Dea not to repeat the howler. The Minister of State assured him that his comments were just top-of-the-head stuff and that he supported the government. But, to the annoyance of the party leadership, O'Dea spoke for a second time on local radio, expressing solidarity with a policy of deregulation with which he said he personally did not agree. This annoyed the Taoiseach further, since O'Dea was 'having it both ways'. It was reported that O'Dea was told to cease his outbursts in favour of taxi drivers or face losing the party whip.

Nor were Fianna Fáil backbenchers impressed. Conor Lenihan, later to become a Minister of State himself, said that if O'Dea was in any other country in the world, 'he would get his marching orders on the spot'. Stating that O'Dea should apologise to the Tanaiste and Bobby Molloy, he said: 'It is simply not appropriate for a serving minister openly to contradict government policy by urging opposition to that policy. It is simply not credible. It is quite different for backbenchers to make noise on an issue. But when a minister takes the seal of office, he or she cannot urge people to fight government policy. You implement policy, not oppose it. Ministers have a huge collective responsibility of loyalty to actively defend the government. The Taoiseach has been very lenient and generous in how he has dealt with Mr O'Dea,' Lenihan said.

During the Dáil debate on the motion, O'Dea stressed he fully supported Government policy on taxi deregulation and apologised to the Taoiseach and the PDs for any embarrassment his pro-taxi driver stand had caused.

He told the Dáil: 'On Thursday night, 23 November, I addressed a large meeting of taxi and hackney drivers in Limerick. I now realise that some of the remarks I made at that meeting were intemperate, insensitive and insulting to my colleagues and I wish to take this opportunity to apologise unreservedly to the Tanaiste and to the other members of the Progressive Democrats, particularly the Minister of State,

Deputy Molloy, for any offence caused. I have always had an excellent working relationship with my Progressive Democrats colleagues and hope that it will continue.'

Crucially for the government and for O'Dea's continued role as a minister, he added that 'whatever my private views on this issue, I fully support Government policy on deregulation. I subscribe fully to the notion of collective responsibility.'

He further conceded that 'having studied Mr Justice Murphy's judgment in full' he now realised that legal constraints prevented the Minister of State Bobby Molloy 'from having one regime for taxis in one area and a different regime in another.'

He also strongly denied he had 'said one thing privately in Limerick and something else publicly in Dublin'. One could also speak publicly in Limerick, he said: 'I cannot understand how addressing a meeting of 400 people in Limerick can be said to be speaking privately.' Neither could he understand how an interview with local radio in Limerick or with the *Limerick Leader* could be said to be private. With regard to his reported remark that he had not known his Limerick speech was being taped, he commented that, 'All I said is that if I had known my remarks were being taped and directly transmitted to the Minister of State, Deputy Molloy and others, I would, of course, have moderated my tone and been less offensive and insulting'.

Although apologetic, O'Dea was also typically combative, challenging Nora Owen of Fine Gael to repeat 'outside the House' her accusation that he had condoned or encouraged illegality. O'Dea said he had taken pains in his speech in Limerick to say he did not condone illegality.

'That section of my speech did not appear in the tape publicised by RTÉ and if I were a person of cynical disposition – which I'm not, even at this stage – I would say the reason

RTÉ omitted this section from its broadcast version is that it would have taken much good out of the story.'

Claiming that 'hypocrisy had permeated this debate from start to finish', O'Dea said one of the first TDs to address a meeting of taxi drivers at the gathering on 28 November was Michael Noonan, of Fine Gael, who was reported in *The Irish Times* as saying Limerick was 'different from Dublin' and a separate case would have to be made for Limerick.

He had not detected any attempt by the Fine Gael leader, John Bruton, to seek Mr Noonan's resignation, O'Dea said.

Neither was there 'one word' in Labour leader Ruairi Quinn's speech about Michael D Higgins' statement 'contradicting Labour Party policy on deregulation', he said.

Of course neither Noonan nor Higgins were ministers at the time they made their remarks and it was not their government overseeing deregulation. Despite his tough words, it was widely believed at the time that one more wrong move from O'Dea would result in him losing his ministry. Hindsight tells us that it may not have been that straightforward. Far from being demoted, within four years of effectively challenging the authority of the government of which he was a member, O'Dea was appointed to the cabinet as Minister for Defence. If the Taoiseach had not changed his mind at the last minute in 2002 and, after intense lobbying, decided to keep Joe Walsh and Michael Smith in the cabinet, O'Dea would have been a full minister even sooner.

Having been a junior minister since the early 1990s, a regular poll topper and one of the hardest-working politicians in the Dáil, few disputed that O'Dea deserved his promotion but he has to consider himself fortunate that his misguided efforts to be all things to all men during the taxi deregulation dispute didn't propel him to the backbenches.

Czech-Mate

Royston Brady

THE BACKGROUND

In early 2004, Royston Brady was well on his way to becoming a household name in Ireland. As Lord Mayor of the capital city, the young Dub was enjoying a profile probably last experienced by the man many regarded (almost certainly incorrectly, as events turned out) as his political mentor, Bertie Ahern, when he was in the Mansion House. As with Bertie, a bigger stage beckoned for Royston and his nomination as a Fianna Fáil candidate in the elections to the European Parliament in the summer seemed set to confirm his elevation as a national political figure.

THE GAFFE

In February – the day before he was nominated as a Fianna Fáil candidate in Dublin – Brady appeared on an RTÉ radio political quiz show, whereupon he was thrown what the

Americans would term a curve ball. The would-be European politician was asked to name the ten states due to join the EU later in the year. A tricky enough test to name all ten, but Brady appeared to be unable to think of one. 'You want the whole ten?' he asked incredulously – before presenter Kay Sheehy effectively let him walk to first base by listing Latvia, Lithuania and Estonia. Brady then came up with Poland, leaving as Sheehy pointed out just six left to name. However, the would-be MEP decided enough was enough. 'I'm not going to get the six. No. I'm not going to . . . Because this will come back to haunt me eventually, so I'll pass.' But not before he had a further stab at the question, incorrectly putting forward Croatia and then rightly choosing the Czech Republic. 'You've got the Czechs as well, have you? . . . So Czechs, Poles . . . Who else have you in there?' Ouch!

THE IMPACT

While the inability to name even a majority of the accession states raised questions about the candidate's suitability as an MEP, the damage to his campaign would probably have been limited. However, the embarrassing incident seemed to many to prompt a major tactical rethink in the Brady campaign. The outspoken, plain-speaking politician – he described his colleagues in Dublin City Council as clowns and accused Justice Minister Michael McDowell of being a bully who had given the two fingers to Dublin – became the Quiet Man, extremely reticent and reluctant to do media interviews. His campaign workers denied he was avoiding interviews but the clear perception was that the media were seeing far less of Brady than

any of the other candidates. *The Last Word* radio show on Today FM certainly thought so, famously labelling him a chicken, complete with chicken sounds, for refusing to be interviewed on the show. Going below the media radar did not pay off. As the *Irish Independent* later noted: 'His decision to play hard to get did nothing but reinforce the view that this man had nothing sensible to say – on Europe or anything else'.

Fairly or unfairly, Brady's campaign was increasingly presented in the media as, according to one commentator, a 'caricature of cynical and manipulative marketing' – all 'posters and joshing encounters in the street. None of that nasty live studio stuff.' However, it was only in the closing stages of his campaign that it became clear that Brady's once high opinion poll rating was seriously slipping. Brady also lacked what every politician needs to succeed, namely luck.

The most serious blow to his chance of victory came when a journalist asked him about an interview he gave to *Hot Press* the previous November in which he spoke of his father's taxi being hijacked by the Dublin-Monaghan bombers in 1974. Due to a lack of any firm evidence and due to Brady's failure to assist the Barron Inquiry (the inquiry set up to investigate the bombings), the widespread belief was that he had made the story up to attract sympathy. As a result, he received an extremely damaging hammering in the media and his campaign descended into high farce.

Unfortunately for Brady, a week after the polls closed it became clear that the story was not, in fact, fabricated. On the very day of the bombings in May 1974, *The Irish Times* reported that two Dublin taxis, one belonging to Brady's father, had been hijacked the previous day. However, by the time the story came out, Brady had lost the election – coming in seventh place in first preference votes and being eliminated on the fifth count. It was all a long way from the predictions months earlier that he would top the poll. 'Royston Brady was disbelieved,' the *Irish Independent* later argued in relation to the taxi story, 'in all probability, because he was publicly perceived as the boy who cried wolf.' The reality was that by the end of the campaign nobody outside his immediate circle really knew Royston Brady. Close colleagues said the image presented by the media was totally unfair. 'Anyone who knows him will tell you that he's not a buffoon, he's not a fool, he's not a twit, he's not a mindless idiot. He's as clever a guy as you and I, and given the opportunity, he would show that. But the media has a need for mythical characters,' one friend was quoted as saying at the time.

But what is undeniable is that the European Election campaign, starting with that quiz show appearance in February 2004, was a disaster for Brady. It started with Brady as a coming force – one of the few politicians in the country widely known by their first name. It ended with text messages poking fun at the way his campaign fell apart. 'Carlsberg don't do running mates,' said one such text. 'But if they did, it would be Royston Brady.'

Still a very young man, it remains to be seen if he has truly walked away from politics. One Labour party veteran was quoted after the election as saying that Brady would find it hard to return. 'I think he will find it hard to recover from the damage of the last couple of weeks. He is, maybe unfairly, now regarded as a sort of joke figure in politics.' However, history shows us the electorate does forgive and forget. Given the profile he was capable of building in such a short time and the colour he brought to the often anonymous Lord Mayor's position, it would probably be premature to rule out a resurrection of his political career.

You, Sir, Are A Waffler!

Bertie Ahern

THE BACKGROUND

Early December 1994 and Irish politics was going through one of its most extraordinary periods in the history of the State. The Albert Reynolds-led coalition of Fianna Fáil and Labour had collapsed due to its botched handling of the extradition of paedophile priest Brendan Smyth and Reynolds' insistence on appointing Attorney General Harry Whelehan as president of the High Court.

A couple of years later, only a handful of those involved could remember why the government collapsed, but the fallout from the controversy was enormous. Reynolds resigned as Taoiseach and as leader of Fianna Fáil. Bertie Ahern succeeded him as leader. Initially, everything pointed to a new Fianna Fáil/Labour coalition with Ahern as Taoiseach, once again leaving John Bruton and Fine Gael 'dead in the water' to quote *The Irish Times'* anonymous columnist Drapier.

However, on Monday, 5 December, just a matter of hours before Labour was due to support Ahern's nomination as

Taoiseach, the party suspended negotiations with Fianna Fáil after a front-page story in *The Irish Times* reopened the controversy surrounding the appointment of Whelehan and the handling of the extradition of Smyth. Suddenly everything changed and Labour began negotiations with Fine Gael and Democratic Left with a view to forming a Rainbow coalition.

This time it was Bertie Ahern, not John Bruton, who was out in the cold. The ultimate prize was snatched away from Ahern at the last moment. With the economy about to experience the most explosive growth in the history of Ireland – something Ahern as Minister for Finance would have been acutely conscious of – and Fianna Fáil being blamed by the public for the whole mess, there was no guarantee that he would ever become Taoiseach. Fergus Finlay, writing in his political memoir, *Snakes & Ladders*, described how even before *The Irish Times'* story broke, Ahern 'seemed tired and weary, and even somewhat down-hearted'. It was little wonder. Tensions within Fianna Fáil were running extremely high and there was division in the party over the conduct of Reynolds and other senior ministers in the aftermath of the collapse of the government. There were conflicting versions of events between Fianna Fáil ministers and the Attorney General Eoghan Fitzsimmons.

Differences were also emerging between Ahern and Reynolds, who was still Acting Taoiseach. In his book, *One Spin on the Merry-Go-Round*, Reynolds' government press secretary Sean Duignan wrote: 'The problem was that a caretaker Taoiseach and the new FF party leader were restlessly prowling around each other. Reynolds still seemed to many to be setting the agenda.' There was criticism of Ahern within the party over his handling of the fallout from the whole affair. The new leader was clearly trying to maintain unity in his party, but many of his supporters wanted him to get everything out in the open rather than use a method described in one newspaper as the 'drip, drip, drip of information'. The new Fianna Fáil leader must have felt that he was caught between a rock and a hard place. Given all the disappointments and pressures bearing down on him, it was little wonder he was about to get uncharacteristically ratty.

On 7 December, the Legislation and Security Select Committee of TDs began its special Dáil investigation into the events surrounding the Brendan Smyth case and its aftermath. There were thirty members of the committee but other TDs had the right to attend and take part in proceedings although they could not vote. Not surprisingly, given the level of interest, the committee sat in the Dáil chamber and hundreds of thousands of people watched on television. It was not Dáil Éireann's finest hour. As soon as the investigation began, there was procedural wrangling about giving 'privilege' to witnesses (witnesses could give evidence without fear of subsequent libel actions) and about compelling witnesses to appear.

Fine Gael levelled accusations that Ahern and the caretaker government were using legal provisions to block the committee's progress. For Ahern, it seemed to be the straw that broke the camel's back. The frustrations of the previous weeks came tumbling out.

THE GAFFE

Ahern did his best to explain why the government felt it had to pass legislation before it could grant 'privilege' to witnesses. After a series of interruptions, Ahern told the committee he was 'going to try to be helpful to Fine Gael but maybe deputy [Gay] Mitchell does not want me to be'. Mitchell responded that he wanted Ahern 'to stop smoke screening'. The Fianna Fáil leader snapped back: 'Nobody is smoke screening. If you stop waffling we might get some work done. You are a waffler. You have been years around here waffling.'

THE IMPACT

Curiously, the following day's newspapers barely referred to Ahern's outburst. *The Irish Times* referred to Ahern's 'brief but truculent appearance'. The *Irish Independent* did use the quote in its colour piece on the proceedings in which it also described Mitchell as having 'spent the day doing an impression of a hen on a hot griddle'. The *Independent*'s editorial described the events at the committee as 'a shambles' and an 'appalling misuse of the Dáil'. The committee had 'degenerated into an out-of-control bad tempered slanging match where not even the normal courtesies of debate were followed,' it said.

Yet long after the committee's investigation and indeed the detail of the whole controversy was forgotten, Ahern's 'waffler' outburst is remembered. As political insults go, levelling the charge at someone of being a waffler is hardly the worst. If Ahern had made the comment in the days before debates were televised, it simply would have not registered in the public consciousness. However, radio and television captured the venom in Ahern's tone and ensured that it would live long in the public memory. While his frustration was understandable given all that had happened in the previous days, it was not the way the new Fianna Fáil leader would have wanted to portray himself. Image-wise, it was a disastrous outburst by Ahern. The following day in the Dáil, he extended an olive branch to Mitchell: 'Yesterday at the select committee my good colleague in the House, Deputy Gay Mitchell, and I exchanged some angry words. As the Deputy well knows, I would not want any rancour . . .', to which Mitchell responded: 'I accept your apology'.

Ahern did fulfil his dream of becoming Taoiseach – in fact he went on to become the second longest-serving Taoiseach in the history of the State – but he was always careful to keep his temper in check during Dáil proceedings from that day on.

Honest Jack and Littlejohn

Jack Lynch

THE BACKGROUND

In August 1973, two brothers – Kenneth and Keith Littlejohn – were given hefty sentences by the Special Criminal Court for their part in the robbery of AIB Bank on Grafton Street, at the time the biggest robbery in the history of the State. Even taking into account the size of the robbery, this was not a straightforward bank heist. The two brothers had fled back to the UK after the robbery. But the Gardaí were quickly on to them – one of the brother's electricity bills was found in the getaway car. They were extradited back to this jurisdiction.

During the extradition proceedings, the brothers argued that they shouldn't be sent back to Ireland because they were acting on behalf of the British Ministry of Defence – in other words, they were spies. As part of their role with the British Secret Intelligence Services, they said, they were under instructions to infiltrate the IRA and they carried out the robbery to discredit the IRA in the Republic (although it should be noted that both brothers had been thieves before becoming agents). Kenneth

Littlejohn also claimed that he had been given instructions by MI6 to assassinate leading republicans – although this is regarded as highly unlikely. Many of the brothers' wilder claims were dismissed.

However, the case did cause serious problems in Anglo-Irish relations, not least because the brothers stated they had made contact with British Defence Minister Lord Carrington and a Junior Minister. British intelligence admitted the two men were agents, but denied that they were authorised to carry out illegal activities. There was already considerable sensitivity about the issue of British agents operating in the Republic. In December 1972, a British agent, John Wyman, had been arrested in a Dublin hotel in the act of receiving confidential documents from a garda sergeant who worked with the Garda security section. Both men were charged with various offences under the Official Secrets Act. Their trial in February 1973 was held *in camera* (i.e. not in open court) and they were ultimately convicted of much less serious charges and quickly released.

There was yet another reason for tension in Anglo-Irish relations. On 2 December, 1972, bomb blasts in Dublin killed two people and injured over seventy. The bombings happened just as the Dáil was about to vote on a draconian Offences against the State (Amendment) Bill. Once the bombs went off, opposition to the bill collapsed and it was widely speculated that British intelligence agents had a hand in the attack. Fianna Fáil leader Jack Lynch, the following year when he was leader of the opposition, voiced his suspicion that the bombings were the work of British intelligence. This was denied by the press office at Number 10, Downing Street.

The extradition case involving the Littlejohn brothers was held *in camera* in Britain but having been sentenced by the

Special Criminal Court in Dublin, the Littlejohn case dominated newspaper headlines in Ireland and Britain. Although nowhere near as serious as the Wyman case – the brothers were no threat to the security of the state – comparisons were (briefly) drawn in Britain with the Watergate scandal which was unfolding in the US. There were calls for the resignation of Lord Carrington and the opposition Labour Party demanded an inquiry. Meanwhile, in Ireland, Lynch in his role as leader of the opposition called on the Irish government to press the British for full disclosure of the facts. The coalition, other than making it known that intelligence activities in the Republic by Britain were unacceptable, said little about the case.

THE GAFFE

It emerged in August 1973 that in early January of that year – two days after the brothers appeared in court in Britain claiming to be British agents and before they were returned to Dublin to answer the bank robbery charges – British government involvement in the case had been admitted to the Fianna Fáil government. Lynch, as leader of the opposition, had been urging full disclosure of the facts, but this revelation begged the question: what had he been doing when he was Taoiseach to get full disclosure in January and February before Fianna Fáil lost the general election? Lynch replied that the only contact between his government and the British government on the Littlejohn affair was a request by the British DPP for an affidavit by the Irish Attorney General that the prosecution against the brothers did not have political implications. This was necessary, Lynch said, for the extradition proceedings. He added that the affidavit was given as there was no indication that the bank robbery had any link with political matters (the Irish government sought an assurance that neither brother had been employed by the UK government to 'subborn' any member of the Irish security forces, i.e that it was not another 'Wyman' case).

However, Lynch was utterly wrong about this being the only contact and to his enormous embarrassment this oversight emerged just a few days later. Foreign Affairs Minister Garret FitzGerald asked the secretary general of his department, Hugh McCann, to ring the Fianna Fáil leader. McCann reminded Lynch that he had brought a report to him from the Irish Ambassador in London, Donal O'Sullivan, in early January containing an admission of official British involvement in the Littlejohn affair. The report said the British government wished to inform the Irish government that one of the Littlejohn brothers had contacted the British Intelligence Service offering information about the IRA and that offer had been accepted. The report went on to say that subsequently the British Intelligence Service received information that the brothers were involved, or might be involved, with the IRA in bank robberies. The Intelligence Service made it clear that if the brothers were involved in such activities, they had no authority from the Service to do so.

THE IMPACT

The revelation was disastrous for Lynch. The front-page headline in *The Irish Times* on 14 August, 1973 read: 'Lynch knew Littlejohns were agents in January' with the sub-heading, 'Documents prove British government's admission to Dublin through ambassador'. Lynch issued a statement from his holiday home near Skibbereen in which he said that he had forgotten about the ambassador's report. Lynch said he had received the report the day before he left for the US on an IDA promotional trip and he asked Hugh McCann to forward it to the Department of Justice. He added that when he had made his statement the previous week saying the only contact had been the British seeking the affadavit: 'I did not recall Mr McCann's visit to me'. He thanked Garret FitzGerald for his courtesy in asking McCann to remind him of the report. But he also stressed that the report made no mention of the British government, or any member of it, having contact with the Littlejohns. Presumably, that would have been fairly unforgettable.

The following day at a press conference in Skibbereen, Lynch said he regarded his lapse 'as serious in the circumstances' and he would have to consider his position as leader of Fianna Fáil. Senior figures in the party rallied around him. Des O'Malley, who as Minister of Justice had also seen the report, tried to take the spotlight off his leader. O'Malley had been on holidays and uncontactable when Lynch made his original statement denying any contact from the British admitting involvement with the Littlejohns. 'I am the principal person to blame. If I had not been on holiday for the past week or so, Mr Lynch would have contacted me and I would have refreshed his memory', he said, adding that everybody had a loss of memory from time to time.

Brian Lenihan, another senior figure, described it as a 'lapse of recollection which did not warrant any action within Fianna Fáil', an interesting choice of words given his infamous 'on mature recollection' comment almost two decades later. An editorial in *The Irish Times* told Lynch to 'forget' any ideas of resigning, advising him to wait for a couple of other resignations, including Lord Carrington's. In the meantime, it said, 'go fishing'. The previous day's editorial had (rather harshly) savaged the coalition government for making 'propaganda at the ineptitude of their predecessors' instead of showing a common front to the UK. There may be more brains on the government benches but there was also 'more ego, more vanity and perhaps more malice', it said, adding: 'smartness is not everything'. The editorial noted that the 'statesmanlike' Lynch, despite internal pressures in his party, had always backed Taoiseach Liam Cosgrave's approach on the North as part of a bipartisan policy and he had received a 'blow below the belt'. Which was most important – it asked – making 'a Scarva sham fight out of the opening which Mr Lynch foolishly left them' or maintaining the healthy bipartisanship towards Britain and the North? The coalition had had its fun, Fianna Fáil was left red-faced, but the country's face was also red, the editorial added. It concluded by suggesting that it would now be more difficult for Cosgrave to face Heath over Littlejohn.

Lynch did not resign, although there seems to be little doubt that he seriously considered it and it was not simply a rallying call to the faithful. However, the groundswell of opinion in his favour convinced him to stay on. Some found it hard to believe that he would have forgotten such important information, but there really is no other logical explanation for his actions. The fact that the Irish government had been informed in January was obviously going to come out, so it would have been crazy for Lynch to try and pretend he had been told nothing about the Littlejohn affair while he was Taoiseach. Garret FitzGerald, though a political rival, certainly believed him. To emphasise the point in his autobiography, he described how at the height of the controversy, he asked his secretary general in the Department of Foreign Affairs if he could see the documents for himself. Hugh McCann replied: 'Oh Minister, don't you remember, I showed them to you in May?' FitzGerald wrote that at this point his sympathy for Lynch increased immeasurably. Noting that Lynch would have been distracted both by his trip to the US and the pending general election, he concluded: 'Under the pressure of events, everybody involved had forgotten what had happened, apart from the vigilant Hugh McCann'.

But despite it being an honest mistake, there is little doubt that Lynch's reputation suffered as a result. 'A degree of fun was poked at him for having forgotten what he had known about the curious incident in Anglo-Irish relations,' FitzGerald said. And TP O'Mahony in his biography of Jack Lynch wrote that the episode weakened Lynch and focused certain minds within Fianna Fáil on the possibility of replacing him. It would take over six years for that to happen, however, and four years after his Littlejohn embarrassment, Lynch handed the 'brainier' coalition parties a thumping electoral defeat.

My (Own) Way

Charlie McCreevy

THE BACKGROUND

By October 1982, Charlie Haughey's notorious GUBU government had been in power as a minority government since the previous March. As the government lurched from one crisis to another, disenchantment with the party leader rose. In February of that year, Fianna Fáil failed for the second time under Haughey to win an overall majority despite the collapse of the Fine Gael/Labour coalition after a hugely unpopular move to introduce a tax on children's shoes.

This failure prompted questions about the leadership of Fianna Fáil in the immediate wake of the election. Moves were made to allow Fianna Fáil TD Des O'Malley to challenge Haughey for the leadership and attempt to become the party's nomination for Taoiseach when the new Dáil began. However, the challenge collapsed ignominiously after Haughey brought forward the Fianna Fáil parliamentary party meeting to confirm his nomination as the party's candidate for Taoiseach. At that meeting, O'Malley announced he was not allowing his name to be proposed as nominee for Taoiseach. According to Raymond Smith's hugely entertaining *Charles J. Haughey: The Survivor*, Charlie McCreevy – once a strong supporter of Haughey who had become an outspoken critic of the leader – went around to Hunter's Pink Elephant bar after the meeting had ended and drank two whiskies. 'He vowed to himself that next time it would be different, because he would organise it himself, and in his own way.' His chance would come the following October as problem after problem beset Haughey and his government.

THE GAFFE

On Friday evening, 1 October, 1982, a friend of McCreevy's, driving a yellow Mercedes, arrived at the Kinsealy home of Haughey and handed in a copy of a no-confidence motion. At the same time, McCreevy's secretary handed the original to government chief whip Bertie Ahern. McCreevy had consulted nobody else about his move – it was a coup planned and executed by one person only. The only other person who knew what he intended to do was his personal secretary who had typed the two copies of the no-confidence motion.

THE IMPACT

O'Malley, who was in Spain on government business, got a phone call in the middle of the night with the news of the challenge. He was furious with McCreevy for acting unilaterally. Years later, he told Stephen Collins, author of

Breaking the Mould – How the PDs Changed Irish Politics: 'Before I went to Spain it had been agreed that nothing of the kind would be done for at least a fortnight. McCreevy's foolish and impetuous action helped Haughey to remain as Fianna Fáil leader for nearly ten years longer than he might have done and the consequences for Ireland were disastrous. Whatever McCreevy did for Ireland as Minister for Finance, he didn't do much for the country in 1982.'

O'Malley was livid that the challenge had been laid down when the anti-Haughey faction of the party was so unprepared. Nevertheless, he felt he had no option but to oppose Haughey. He and another government minister, Martin O'Donoghue, resigned from the cabinet and along with former Tanaiste and long-time Haughey rival George Colley made a determined effort to oust Haughey. However, Haughey, who insisted on an open vote despite McCreevy's statement that there should be a secret ballot, defeated the motion by 58 votes to 22.

O'Malley's assertion that McCreevy's action helped Haughey to remain on for another decade is by no means certain. Given the fact that four months later, at the height of the hugely damaging phone-tapping scandal, Haughey was able – albeit by a very narrow margin – to survive a further attempt to depose him suggests that no amount of combined advance planning would have toppled Haughey in what was termed the 'October Revolution'.

McCreevy's motivation was understandable. He was disgusted at the haphazard nature of the February 1982 challenge and this time was determined to push things. 'The Kildare deputy decided that next time round he would do the job himself. He thought up a plan of his own. He worked it all out and typed it out on sheets of paper – every stage of the plan. He planned carefully what actions he would take – step by step – and he even wrote down what response he expected to each step from Haughey,' Raymond Smith wrote in his book. The key to the entire plan, Smith added, was that there would be no inkling of what was to come until the copies of the no-confidence motion were handed in at Kinsealy and Government Buildings. Once Haughey knew that McCreevy was personally behind the motion, he would know that it would be a fight to the finish.

While McCreevy's plan failed, Smith wrote that after the vote the Kildare TD felt like a man who had been a member of an All Ireland winning team. 'As McCreevy saw it, it was all about redeeming honour after the manner in which the February bid had failed. He had seen twenty-two people showing the guts to stand up and declare their hand in front of Charles Haughey – 22 had stood up and were counted in an open vote.'

Years later, it was clear that McCreevy still believed he did the right thing. 'I didn't care. This time there was going to be a vote and we weren't going to back off. We'd know for once and for all,' he said.

Certainly nobody could doubt McCreevy's sheer guts in doing what he did. Along with other members of the 'Club of 22', McCreevy received some rough treatment in the car park of Leinster House on the night of the parliamentary party meeting. He was chased across the car park, kicked and jostled and called a 'bastard' and a 'blueshirt'. Gardaí helped McCreevy to get into his car, and as he drove away, a crowd surrounded it, banging on the roof and shouting insults.

McCreevy stood up for his principles and remained on the backbenches for another decade for doing so, but it is hard to see how he thought his solo run was going to help bring Haughey down.

Rambo Killed the Radio Star
Ray Burke

THE BACKGROUND

In the late 1980s and early 1990s, Ray 'Rambo' Burke, Minister for Communications in successive Fianna Fáil governments, oversaw a revolution in Irish broadcasting. He established the new Independent Radio and Television Commission (IRTC), which in turn licensed a new national independent radio station and 25 new local radio stations. Although reform of the broadcasting sector was long overdue, it was much commented upon that Burke had – in unprecedented fashion – kept the Communications portfolio as he moved through three different departments: Energy, Industry and Commerce, and Justice.

His tenure in Communications was highly controversial. In fact, a decade later, it came under the close scrutiny of the Flood Tribunal. While Burke insisted he wanted to create choice and a level playing pitch for all broadcasters, his opponents accused him of bias and cronyism. The opposition claimed the Minister was seeking to do 'irreparable damage to RTÉ by hook or by crook' because of Montrose's critical coverage of the government during elections. There seems little doubt that Burke did have a major antipathy towards RTÉ, believing, as one commentator wrote, that it was 'full of 'Stickies' with an 'innately anti-Fianna Fáil' editorial philosophy.

In January 1989, the IRTC chose Century – controlled by concert promoter and lifelong Fianna Fáil supporter Oliver Barry and businessman James Stafford – for the national licence. The station's start-up was delayed over a dispute with RTÉ concerning transmission fees. In March of that year, Burke intervened to force RTÉ to drop its asking price by a third, effectively saving the new station almost IR£200,000. It emerged afterwards that in May 1989, Barry gave Burke IR£35,000 to help with election expenses. The contracts for Century Radio were signed in July and the station went on air in September. However, the new station, bereft of listeners and advertising revenue, quickly ran into financial difficulties.

THE GAFFE

The following year, Burke made a second key intervention aimed at encouraging broadcasting alternatives to RTÉ and 'levelling the playing field' in relation to the edge which the licence fee gave RTÉ over its new competition. He proposed that IR£3 million of the IR£45 million RTÉ received at the time from licence fees would be distributed among independent radio stations, to take account of the 20% of their output which they had to devote to news, current affairs and community service programmes. Much more controversially, he announced that

RTÉ's second radio station, 2FM, would not continue as a pop music station.

Burke claimed that 2FM had served its purpose, which was to provide a service that the pirate stations prior to its establishment had been exclusively delivering. This was no longer needed because the independents were up and running. Instead, he proposed that the station would become more educational in format 'more in keeping with the public service mandate of RTÉ'. It would be up to the RTÉ Authority to draw up plans for an alternative use of the network. However, Burke let it be known that he envisaged the revamped 2FM carrying European language courses – 'particularly important' in the run-up to the Single Market – Irish language courses and information for farmers, businessmen and trade unionists 'as well as a range of special interest and specialist music areas'. It was, one commentator later wrote, an effort to turn 2FM into 'the equivalent of Albanian state radio' – though perhaps not quite as interesting.

THE IMPACT

Burke may have had a point as to whether public service broadcasting extended to a pop music channel. He may also have been right about the absence of a level playing field. But, politically, his intervention was disastrous. The outrage of the opposition was hardly unexpected, but the government was taken aback by the huge backlash from the general public. This was in evidence when the Gay Byrne radio show on RTÉ Radio One asked listeners to phone in their views. There was a huge response and the reaction was eight to one against any changes.

Burke's timing was lousy. The station had endured a pretty rocky beginning after it was launched – with what Gerry Ryan described as 'very, very indecent haste' – as Radio 2 in 1979 by a reluctant government, which wanted a spoiler to the popular pirates. The real turning point in its fortunes came with a revamp in 1987 which gave Ryan a central role with a new morning show. By the time Burke tried to get rid of it, the station had become genuinely popular, particularly among younger listeners. Public opinion was firmly behind the station's DJs. Burke, arriving at Montrose for a meeting, was greeted by employees who lined the avenue and gave him a slow handclap all the way. He was not impressed, but the public were. A record was recorded to the tune of Billy Joel's *We didn't start the fire* with lyrics defending 2FM.

Fianna Fáil TDs across the country were being told by their constituents: 'hands off 2FM'. There was a growing sense of unease within the Fianna Fáil coalition about the reaction, with a number of meetings between the two party leaders. Fianna Fáil didn't become the most dominant political party in western Europe by ignoring that level of public outrage and the proposal was quickly dumped. Instead, Burke introduced a Broadcasting Bill which set a cap on RTÉ's revenue and proposed the diversion of up to IR£6m to commercial broadcasting. RTÉ, understandably, was not pleased, but 2FM was safe.

Inevitably, the question has been asked over the years as to whether Burke – in the words of Pat Rabbitte in the Dáil in 2000 – 'sought to relegate 2FM at that time to clear the pitch for Century Radio'. Burke always denied that the timing of his broadcasting bill had anything to do with Century's financial problems.

Rabbitte also recalled in that Dáil speech an incident, recounted by the head of news at Capital Radio at the time, in which Burke threw a 'tantrum' when he heard the new Dublin radio station broadcast comments by Workers' Party TD Eamon Gilmore in its first news bulletin. Out of earshot he told the news editor: 'Did you not know that one of the reasons we set up these new stations was to get people like that off the air?' Rabbitte noted that 'Burke then proceeded to cancel Capital's derogation from the 20% news requirement.'

Burke's actions in capping RTÉ's revenue wasn't enough to save Century, which eventually folded in November 1991.

Over a decade later, the Flood Tribunal found that the directive obliging RTÉ to provide its facilities to Century in March 1989 was 'issued to advance the private interests of the promoters of Century and not to serve the public interest'. It also found the payment of IR£35,000 to Burke by Barry in May 1989 was 'a corrupt payment made in response to a demand for £30,000 cash by Mr. Burke, and was not intended by Mr. Barry to be a political donation to Mr. Burke or to Fianna Fáil'. Furthermore, 'in proposing legislation which would have had the effect of curbing RTÉ's advertising, altering the format of 2FM, and diverting broadcasting licence fee income from RTÉ to independent broadcasters, Mr. Burke was acting in response to demands made of him by the promoters of Century and was not serving the public interest,' the report found.

The listeners of 2FM could have told anybody that more than a decade earlier.

The Three Houses
Padraig 'Pee' Flynn

THE BACKGROUND

It was January 1999 and former Fianna Fáil Minister Padraig
Flynn was six years into his job as European Commissioner
with responsibility for Social Affairs. During his tenure, he had
surprised his many critics in Ireland by bringing an enlightened
approach to his portfolio and he was widely regarded as one of
the most effective commissioners in Brussels. However, trouble
was brewing over allegations that he had received IR£50,000
from property developer Tom Gilmartin while Minister for
Environment in the late 1980s.

THE GAFFE

As the song goes, it happened on the *Late Late Show*. During his
interview, Flynn generally came across as eccentric and out-of-
touch. He managed to infuriate Tom Gilmartin with comments

about Gilmartin's health – and that of his wife. He also angered many of the watching audience by complaining about the difficulties of living on 'just' IR£100,000 a year.

Asked by Gay Byrne if he knew Gilmartin, Flynn said: 'Yeah, I haven't seen him now for some years. I met him. He's a Sligo man who went to England and made a lot of money. Came back. Wanted to do a lot of business in Ireland. Didn't work out for him. He's not well. His wife isn't well. And he's out of sorts.' A woman claiming to be Gilmartin's sister contacted the show and insisted that Flynn's comments about Gilmartin were factually incorrect. Flynn had already left the studio so the show's producers contacted his daughter, Beverley Cooper-Flynn. She managed to make contact with her father, who agreed to issue an apology for his comments. At the end of the show, Byrne told his viewers, 'In the interview it was suggested by Pee Flynn that Tom Gilmartin was sick. As far as Pee is concerned, Tom Gilmartin is not sick and has never been seriously sick and we would just like to say sorry and apologise for that.' But for Flynn the damage was done.

His comments about the difficulties of maintaining three houses, cars and housekeepers on an EU Commissioner's salary also attracted enormous public scorn.

THE IMPACT

Difficult to know where to start as the fallout was enormous. For Flynn personally, it killed off any hopes of being reappointed for a third time as European Commissioner. Tanaiste Mary Harney described his position as 'impossible', although he survived until the following September. His tenure ended when the entire EU Commission resigned. The Gilmartin revelations also closed off a Peter Sutherland/Ray McSharry style career serving on company boards.

Gilmartin was infuriated by the remarks. Although he had been a previously reluctant witness, he said that because of Flynn's comments he would give evidence to the Flood Tribunal on planning which 'will explode at the heart of the current government'. Gilmartin also called on Flynn to resign as EU Commissioner, adding that his remarks on the *Late Late Show* were scurrilous, distressing and inaccurate. He added that Flynn had contacted him repeatedly after media reports of his allegation about the payment surfaced the previous September.

The fallout from the interview dominated politics for weeks, with a motion being passed in the Dáil demanding that Flynn make a 'full immediate statement' clarifying his position in relation to 'the allegations that he had received IR£50,000'. His daughter, Beverley Cooper-Flynn, then a Fianna Fáil TD, voted against the motion and, as a result, she was expelled from the Fianna Fáil parliamentary party (although she was later readmitted).

Gilmartin did give evidence to the Flood Tribunal and while predictions that it would seriously damage Bertie Ahern proved wide of the mark, it did result in a bruising day in the witness box for the Taoiseach.

Flynn's infamous comment about the difficulties of maintaining three houses would later inspire an hilarious spoof letter to a national newspaper from a 'Mr Guyes Bagues', with the address: 'Rue de la Trois Maison', Brussels.

It's Now or Never

Charlie Haughey

THE BACKGROUND

In the 1987 general election, Charlie Haughey failed for the fourth time to deliver an overall majority for Fianna Fáil, despite the massive unpopularity of the outgoing coalition of Fine Gael and Labour. The success of his old rivals in the Progressive Democrats, who won 14 seats, prevented Haughey from achieving his goal. Instead, Haughey formed a minority government that was to prove hugely successful in turning around the country's economy. Although his 1987 general election campaign posters had warned that health cuts 'hurt the old, the sick and the handicapped', Haughey did an about-turn when he entered government.

With Ray McSharry as Finance Minister, Fianna Fáil took serious remedial action to address the chronic state of the public finances. This involved major cuts in public spending, but the minority government was able to survive in the Dáil because, as part of Alan Dukes' Tallaght Strategy, Fine Gael had offered to support it as long as it adhered to strict control of the public finances. Despite the harsh medicine, the government's tough line went down a treat with voters and Fianna Fáil's ratings in the opinion polls were consistently well over 50%. Haughey, himself, enjoyed a voter approval rating in the high sixties. In April of 1989, Haughey returned from an official visit to Japan and was furious to discover the government was about to be defeated in a Dáil private member's motion calling for the allocation of IR£400,000 to help counter the problems of haemophiliacs who been infected with the AIDS virus through bloods supplied by the Irish Blood Transfusion Service.

THE GAFFE

Instead of swallowing hard and accepting the reverse in the Dáil vote, Haughey – urged on by his closest associates in cabinet, Padraig Flynn and Ray Burke – gambled big time and opted to use the government's defeat as an excuse to go to the country. He called a general election to coincide with the European Elections already scheduled for June 1989.

THE IMPACT

Disaster for Fianna Fáil. Far from winning the much sought-after overall majority, Fianna Fáil actually lost four seats after a difficult election campaign dominated by arguments over the cutbacks in health – arguments which the party seemed ill-equipped to deal with. The result meant the party was not even in a position to form a minority government. To stay in power and avoid another general election, Haughey had to break with what was seen as a core Fianna Fáil value by opting to enter into government with his old nemesis Des O'Malley and the PDs.

The election setback and the decision to go into government with the PDs undermined Haughey's authority. Two and a half years later, when fresh controversy emerged over the phone-tapping scandal of 1982, Haughey's fate was effectively determined by the PDs. Former Justice Minister Sean Doherty said that Haughey was fully aware that two journalists' phones were being tapped. It is doubtful whether Haughey would have survived the revelations even if there had been a single party Fianna Fáil government in place – he was certainly coming to the end of his leadership anyway. However, it must have been particularly galling for him as the PDs made it clear that the price of their continued participation in government was Haughey's departure. Rather than dissolve the Dáil and force another election, Haughey made up his mind to step down.

The reasons behind his decision to go to the country in the summer of 1989 when his government was performing so well remain a subject for debate among political commentators. Clearly the prize of an overall majority was an alluring one and with 54% support for Fianna Fáil in the opinion polls, a seemingly attainable one. With the PDs struggling in the opinion polls, the prospect of wiping out the arch-enemy must have also been a factor. Ironically, Haughey's decision to go into government with the PDs ultimately guaranteed the small party a long-term future – despite their dreadful election performance in 1989 in which they lost eight seats.

Some commentators have also speculated that Haughey knew the decision to provide state insurance cover on beef exports to Iraq was proving disastrous and that it was only a matter of time before it became a massive story. The view goes that as a minority government, Haughey would find it hard to ride out the storm – hence the anxiety to attain an overall majority. And, of course, we now also know that Haughey, Burke and Flynn all used the 1989 election campaign to raise enormous sums of money for their own personal use from a variety of wealthy Fianna Fáil supporters. Could the fundraising potential of an election campaign have been a factor in the decision to go to the country?

Whatever the reasons, matters were not helped by the fact that Haughey had to wait a few weeks after the Dáil defeat to call a general election. The European Elections were already pencilled in for 15 June, effectively forcing Haughey to hold the general election on that date. To do otherwise would have prompted major criticism about wasting taxpayers' money on two election days while penny pinching on the highly deserving haemophiliacs issue. Haughey dissolved the Dáil on 25 May, but there had been weeks of media speculation since the Dáil defeat in April and the opposition parties were well prepared for the election, including Fine Gael and the PDs. Just two days into the campaign these two parties announced they had done a deal to form an alternative government. As it turned out, the two parties didn't come remotely close to winning enough seats to form a government.

In the meantime, Fianna Fáil seemed content to fight the election on the basis of its record over the previous two years. It wasn't enough and the reverses suffered in the election changed the Irish political landscape forever. Ironically, although the decision to call an election worked out badly for Haughey, being forced to go into coalition was probably one of the best things that ever happened to Fianna Fáil. Although its core vote would continue to decline, the party was able to stay in government for all but two and a half of the following 18 years.

Good Sports in Fianna Fáil

Albert Reynolds and Michael O'Kennedy

THE BACKGROUND

On 17 September, 1997, the Fianna Fáil parliamentary party met to select a candidate to contest the following month's presidential election. There were suggestions of an 'anyone but Albert' campaign by senior figures in the party amid concerns that former Taoiseach Albert Reynolds would not be able to defeat Labour's declared candidate, Adi Roche. However, Reynolds was the red-hot favourite to win the FF nomination. The other two candidates were former minister and EU Commissioner Michael O'Kennedy and virtual political unknown Professor Mary McAleese.

THE GAFFE

McAleese did not have an agreed proposer or seconder at the parliamentary party meeting. Protocol dictated that a person who was not proposed or seconded could not address the meeting. If that protocol had been invoked, McAleese's presidential aspirations would have been finished. However, according to *The Road from Ardoyne: The Making of a President* by Ray Mac Manais, the other two candidates agreed to waive the need for McAleese to have a proposer or a seconder, following quick consultations with Fianna Fáil chairman Rory O'Hanlon. McAleese was allowed to make what was commonly regarded as a powerful speech at the meeting and she stunned everybody – except, the conspiracy theorists would have it, Bertie Ahern – by defeating Reynolds by 62 votes to 48 in the second ballot and emerging from the meeting with the Fianna Fáil nomination.

But was it a gaffe by McAleese's two rivals for the nomination or simply a case of good sportsmanship on the part of two distinguished politicians more concerned about the spirit than the letter of the rules and anxious to win fair and square? In Mac Manais' book, McAleese herself recalled: 'Either of the candidates could have got rid of me, there and then. They would have been perfectly within their rights to insist that we follow the rules. That would have been the end of me and I would not have been a threat to whichever one of them was elected. I was very grateful for their generosity.'

Her husband Martin, however, was more direct in his comments. 'When Rory O'Hanlon told us about the new procedure, I couldn't believe that Albert had left the door open for her like that. I can only put it down to overconfidence on his part. If I was in his shoes, I'm afraid I would have insisted on party rules being obeyed,' he said.

THE IMPACT

Who knows what would have happened if the party rules had been obeyed? Reynolds would probably have won the nomination and the ensuing presidential election would have been completely open – recent political history may have been a lot different. Instead, McAleese came through a stormy presidential campaign to comfortably win the election. Hugely popular with the electorate, she was returned unopposed seven years later for a second term in the Áras. The election of McAleese was also a massive boost to Bertie Ahern's new coalition government which had endured a rocky first few months in office.

Jacob's Iodine

Joe Jacob

THE BACKGROUND

On 11 September, 2001, co-ordinated terrorist attacks on New York City and Washington DC in America killed thousands of people. The appalling carnage, captured live on television, shocked and saddened the world. There was a state of high alert throughout the western world amid fears of further attacks. Despite Ireland's neutrality, tensions were raised here as to whether we could be victim to a biological, chemical or nuclear attack due to the country's close ties to the US and proximity to Britain – a strong ally of the US.

Researchers on the Marian Finucane morning show on RTÉ Radio One had major difficulty identifying the appropriate government department responsible for drawing up a response strategy in the event of such an attack. Junior Minister Joe Jacob, who was responsible for emergency planning in the event of a national disaster, contacted the show and offered to come in to talk about the issue. According to the Minister, this would help to 'reassure people and let them know that there is in place a national emergency plan for nuclear accidents', which he said was state of the art' and among the best in Europe.

THE GAFFE

However, the interview proved anything but reassuring as the Minister appeared unable to give any details of how the authorities would handle an attack. Jacob opened in very general terms by saying that 'immediately in the aftermath of the atrocity of the 11 September, the Taoiseach put in place a co-ordinating committee involving a range of departments and they are meeting daily and dealing with that. We are not in an emergency situation as we speak, and may it continue, but we must be prepared, so that is why my department has been preparing this plan, updating it, upgrading it, so we have what we have now.'

He said the emergency plan was complete and would be tested in a simulated exercise in the coming fortnight. Within weeks of that, a fact sheet would be sent to 'every home in Ireland' and 'that has been planned for two years'. So far, so good . . . until Finucane started to probe for details of the emergency plan and asked what the nation should do in the immediate aftermath of an instant attack. 'A public awareness campaign, specifically what to do, would be triggered in the immediate aftermath,' he said. Finucane continued to probe: 'Supposing it happened now, what do people do?' The Minister responded: 'First of all, the objective of the plan, it's designed to deal with the incident which you describe and it's overseen by a ministerial committee'. Again Finucane asked: 'But what would we do now?' Jacob replied: 'What we would do now is, first of all an early warning system would tell us and we have that early warning system set up at a number of stages. First of all in Ireland, we have our own network of radiation monitors around the country and they will tell us automatically that they have detected an increase in radiation in the air initially and in the water. That will trigger off alarms and those are manned on a 24-hour basis. Before it arrives we have to make provision as well, so we have international warning agreements with international organisations, and countries that detect an emergency will alert us,' he said.

Later in the interview, asked about the threat of biological or chemical warfare, Jacob said: 'First of all, Marian, I am very qualified to talk to you about nuclear issues and I have done so and I hope it has had the desired effect. I am not qualified to talk to you about what the question you have asked except to say that . . . first of all it's highly unlikely and it was considered highly unlikely that as a small nuclear [sic] country Ireland would be targeted in such a way.' When Finucane interjected that she presumed he meant neutral, rather than nuclear, Jacob agreed: 'I beg your pardon, I have got nuclear on the brain now, a small neutral country.'

He went on to say that an early warning to the Gardaí from international sources would take place in minutes and that information would then be passed to the public in a means described 'on my fact sheet' and 'in the event of this happening all kind of media information will be issued immediately, Marian, the minute it becomes available,' he said. By this stage, Finucane had the bit between her teeth: 'Yeah, what advice?' she asked. 'We're eight minutes on now. What should I have said to the listeners?'

Jacob's response was again notably short on specifics: 'Well, that information will issue based on the technical expertise or not that will assess the situation when it happens, the scale of the incident, the potential of the incident deteriorating or whatever,' he said.

Finucane then asked that if a plane crashed into Sellafield and the wind was blowing our way, what advice would be given to citizens.

Jacob tried in vain to keep to the facts (sheet). 'I'm telling you that, if a plane crashed into Sellafield, we're talking about a very, very major accident there, something like a great power like the United States aren't geared to cope with last week. So we would tell people the situation and they would know from again this famous fact sheet that I'm talking about.'

Again Finucane cut to the chase: 'Well, tell me what to do. You're going to give me the fact sheet in a couple of weeks time and I'll read it, but I'm talking now, it happened nine minutes ago.' She further asked: 'Do I tell those kids on a school bus to turn back home? Do I tell people to stay indoors?'

A struggling Jacob responded: 'Alright, Marian, I'll tell you what you would do. We would say please remain indoors with your doors and windows closed. Switch off your ventilation systems. We want to minimise your levels of exposure to the levels of radiation that are now, God forbid, out of doors. Sheltering is most likely to be appropriate. The next thing is restriction of consumption of contaminated water or foods. Also bringing cattle indoors and using stored animal feeds.' He also added – not very reassuringly – that non-radioactive iodine tablets that reduce the uptake of radioactive iodine following post-nuclear exposure will eventually be available from the Department of Health.

'But how could people get hold of these?' asked Finucane. 'That's one of the things that has to be tweaked in the coming weeks. That will be in the fact sheet when you get it. We mustn't be alarmistic,' Jacob added.

Finucane wasn't impressed: 'The phones upstairs are going bananas. Minister, here we are now, we're 15 minutes into my warning and how do I get my iodine tablet? Tell me.'

Jacob replied: 'You'll get them from the Department of Health and Children and they will be maintaining stocks for that purpose. As soon as you need them. You'll be told when we're in an emergency. We're not in an emergency. That is one of the finer points to be decided.'

THE IMPACT

The fallout was both chemical and nuclear for the government, raising huge questions about the government's state of readiness to deal with an attack. RTÉ reported hundreds of calls from people complaining about Jacob's performance. One caller said: 'If this is the best the country can produce to devise any sort of early-warning plan then we are in serious trouble.' Another memorably described the interview as confirming the government's response to an attack was to 'stick your head between your legs and kiss your ass goodbye'.

One columnist in *The Irish Times* wrote that 'RTÉ reversed years of low-grade comedy programming with a cracker of a confrontation between Marian Finucane and Joe Jacob, Minister of State for Energy. Rumours that the script was written by the Father Ted team soon bit the dust, however, when Bertie Ahern moved to undercut Mr Jacob's extraordinary improvisation'. Ouch!

Nor were the opposition sparing. Fine Gael's Charlie Flanagan called for Jacob's dismissal because of his 'disgraceful show of incompetence' during the interview. 'Instead of conveying clear and concise information on what action the public needs to take in the event of a nuclear disaster, Mr Jacob ended up frightening more people than he reassured,' Flanagan said.

Labour Party TD Emmet Stagg said it was 'blatantly obvious' Jacob had no understanding of his portfolio and described the Minister's performance as 'worthy of a Bull Island sketch'.

While the government sent out Health Minister Mícheál Martin on RTÉ's *Six One News* to ease public fears about the government's readiness to cope in the event of a terrorist attack, a government spokesman insisted Jacob retained the full confidence of the Taoiseach. 'He is doing a great job. He has organised all of this work to review the national emergency plan. The fact that he did not do a good interview – in the view of some people – should not be a reason for him to go,' the spokesman said.

Government sources complained privately that Jacob had told the programme that he could only deal with questions about the State's emergency plans for a nuclear disaster, and not those about germ or biological warfare.

Taoiseach Bertie Ahern later defended his minister but conceded that the interview did not inspire public confidence. He said that Jacob had a bad day and he admitted that he's had those days himself. Ahern argued that Jacob had a vast knowledge of procedures in the event of a nuclear attack and never claimed to be an expert on biological or chemical attacks.

In *The Irish Times,* the anonymous columnist Drapier, writing the following Saturday, probably best summed up the whole affair. 'The first thing people expect of their leaders in times of crisis is reassurance. People need to feel they are safe, that those in charge know what they are doing, that plans are in place, in other words that those elected to lead are competent and sure. It is precisely for these reasons that Joe Jacob's performance was so serious.'

Drapier continued: 'It takes a certain genius to become a household name in the space of half an hour but that is precisely what Joe managed to do. No advertising campaign could do for iodine tablets in a year what Joe did in 30 minutes and the word 'fact sheet' has taken on comic connotations which even the late Dermot Morgan would have envied.

'This was *Bull Island, Scrap Saturday* and *Hall's Pictorial Weekly* all rolled into one. It was welcome light relief after the gloom of the past fortnight, and if, as *Dublin Opinion* used say 'humour was the safety valve of the nation', then we were all safe.'

But, more seriously, Drapier noted that 'the fact was that the interview scared and angered people, probably in equal proportions. If phone calls to radio shows and newspapers are anything to go by, many mothers in particular were deeply upset. Their fears may be irrational but they are real. Many have direct experience of children upset and traumatised by the television pictures of the attack on America and wanted more than bureaucratic talk of co-ordination, interdepartmental task forces and the like, not to mention iodine tablets and fact sheets.'

Drapier argued that the interview was the 'public manifestation of a deeper incompetence, an absence of any sense of reality and an insensitivity to public fears on a fairly major scale', adding that it would be unfair to scapegoat Jacob as there was a 'scramble to pass the buck among government departments'.

There was a sting in the tail for the government when Micheál Martin, in damage limitation mode, told RTÉ's *Morning Ireland* radio show that iodine tablets were stocked in all health boards and there were sufficient stocks. But to add to the sense of farce and to the government's embarrassment it later emerged that many health boards did not have any stocks of tablets. While they had been issued since 1991, as part of the National Nuclear Emergency Plan, they had passed their use-by-date and in some cases had been destroyed. The Department of Health issued a clarifying statement that it was currently finalising arrangements for the purchase of new stocks of iodine tablets for predistribution in the event of a national nuclear emergency. Tablets were subsequently sent to each home in the country.

Jacob, meanwhile, stayed on as Minister for State in the Department of Public Enterprise. However, it was no surprise that he was not reappointed as a junior minister nine months later when the government was returned to power after the May 2002 general election.

The Rubbish Skip

Progressive Democrats

THE BACKGROUND

It was coming up to Christmas 1997 and the Progressive Democrats had endured a difficult year. A disastrous general election campaign (see Chapter 63) almost wiped out the party, but a silk purse was made out of a sow's ear when, despite being returned with just four TDs, the party fortuitously ended up in government with Fianna Fáil. Meanwhile, more mundane housekeeping was going on at the PDs' headquarters, just around the corner from Dáil Eireann on South Frederick Street. As part of a clear out, a skip was left outside their building, in which to deposit unwanted material.

THE GAFFE

Inadvertently, highly sensitive financial documents ended up being thrown into the skip. The documents were discovered by somebody and sent by courier to the offices of the *Sunday Business Post*. Christmas came early that year for the newspaper as the documents – which belonged to former leader Des O'Malley and had been transferred from his ministerial office to the PD headquarters for safekeeping when the party left government in 1992 – detailed the PDs' fundraising over a seven-year period.

THE IMPACT

On the 14 December, the *Sunday Business Post* splashed the story and a giant-sized headline: 'Secret trail of PD funds laid bare by dumped documents' onto the front page. The exclusive news story, backed up inside with three pages of analysis, was massively embarrassing for the PDs as it revealed details of dozens upon dozens of donors to the party. 'Reading like a who's who of the Irish business community, the intimate finances of the PDs over a five year period illustrate the huge financial support enjoyed by [Des] O'Malley and his colleagues,' the report said. Those who made donations included the Smurfit Group, Larry Goodman, Peter McAleer – Des O'Malley's brother-in-law – Irish Distillers, Sisks, O'Flaherty Holdings, Mark Kavanagh of the Custom House Docks Development Company, Tony Ryan of GPA, Neil McCann of Fyffes and Tim O'Mahony of Toyota.

The newspaper also gave details of a letter in 1992 'from prominent solicitor and party fundraiser, Paul Smithwick, to Des O'Malley, then Minister for Industry and Commerce', which 'refers to a 'confidential meeting' between [Michael]

Smurfit and the PD leader in January of that year'. Enclosed with the letter was a copy of a cheque donation of IR£30,000 to the party from the Jefferson Smurfit Group. 'Michael will prove to be an extremely good supporter of the party and I cannot tell you how appreciative he was for our confidential meeting in January,' Smithwick wrote.

It is important to stress that there was nothing wrong with any of these businesses or people making donations to the PDs – all the main political parties raise funds in this way. However, it was still highly embarrassing for the PDs to have, what the *Sunday Business Post* described as, 'nothing less than the entrails of the party' exposed in this manner. 'File after file detailed the names of contributors to the PDs from their foundation in the mid 1980s to 1992 when they left Albert Reynolds' administration,' the newspaper's political editor wrote. Included were photocopies of cheques, receipts, 'groveling letters of thanks and supplication', details of fund-raising dinners and golf classics complete with 'notes to O'Malley from advisers suggesting possible chat-up lines for the bigger players'.

The reaction in the party was one of horror that such sensitive details had been disclosed. Party leader and Tanaiste Mary Harney was hosting a dinner party in her home on the Saturday night that weekend when she got a call from her advisor telling her that he had just received a call from a journalist that the party's financial details were revealed in the *Sunday Business Post*. A guest at the party left to buy an early edition of the paper and returned to Harney's house where they all pored over the coverage. O'Malley himself was reported to be barely able to speak from shock when he was informed what had happened. Colleagues later reported that he was not angry but upset. The daily newspapers were all over the story the following day. The

PDs issued a statement in which it said that it was 'normal and proper' for the Minister of Industry and Commerce to meet with Smurfit as O'Malley had done 'with many other industrialists' during his time in office.

Party senator John Dardis was appointed to get to the bottom of what had happened but nobody ever discovered who threw the files away. Two possible explanations emerged: one was that painters had accidentally thrown out the files; the second was that a party worker, fed up with the clutter in a downstairs office, threw them into the skip. Either way there was 'no suggestion of malicious intent'.

In the end, the controversy did not amount to much. Political reaction was limited. There were a few digs across the floor of Dáil Eireann but all the parties were aware that there but for the grace of God went they. According to *Breaking the Mould: How the PDs Changed Irish Politics*, Stephen Collins' definitive book on the PDs, a devastated O'Malley subsequently wrote to all the people on the list apologising for the incident but many wrote back saying they were honoured to be included among the party supporters.

While some of those named were upset, party trustee Paul Mackay told Collins that 'it was one of those things that was not nearly as damaging as we all thought at the time'. A few days after the story broke, Mary Harney was asked if 1997 had been the party's *annus horribilis*. The Tanaiste laughed. The answer to the question was just too obvious.

17

Rocking the Foundations

Pat Rabbitte

THE BACKGROUND

It was the 16 November, 1994 and the Dáil was experiencing one of its most dramatic days since the Arms Trial almost a quarter of a century earlier. The Fianna Fáil-Labour government had been under strain for some weeks over Taoiseach Albert Reynolds' move to appoint his Attorney General (AG) Harry Whelehan as President of the High Court, despite opposition from Labour. Now the government was on the verge of collapse over the handling of the Fr Brendan Smyth extradition case. There had been a delay of seven months in processing the Smyth extradition warrant in the office of the AG. Wild and unsubstantiated rumours swept through Leinster House as to the reasons behind that long delay. One of the unfounded rumours was that the AG's office had received a letter from a senior figure in the Catholic Church which contributed to the delay in the Smyth case.

THE GAFFE

Pat Rabbitte, then a member of the Democratic Left Party, got up to speak in the Dáil during a procedural discussion on the Order of Business. He asked: 'Will the Taoiseach and the Tanaiste say if, in respect of the recent discovery of documents in the Attorney General's office, there is another document that ought to be before this House that will rock the foundations of this society to its very roots?' Rabbitte added: 'If there is such a document as suggested, its contents should be before this House before Deputy [John] Bruton moves his motion [of no confidence in the government] and we should know now whether the Labour Party has rowed in behind the Taoiseach following the discovery of this document.'

THE IMPACT

The effect on what was already a highly charged atmosphere was sensational. Rabbitte's dramatic use of vocabulary and the suggestion that the very foundations of society would be rocked suggested scandal on an unprecedented level.

Rabbitte's party leader Proinsias de Rossa also waded in. 'It seems that we are dealing with one of the most sleazy events in Irish parliamentary history. Is it true a memorandum has been found in the Attorney General's Office which indicates that there was outside interference in the decision by the Attorney General not to proceed with extradition for seven months?'

The problem for Rabbitte and the Democratic Left was that it quickly became apparent that there was no evidence that any such letter or document existed or had ever existed.

In his immediate response to Rabbitte in the Dáil, Taoiseach Albert Reynolds said his efforts to get to the root of complaints about 'documents that are supposed to exist in the Attorney General's office' had drawn a blank. 'I understand that one of the stories doing the rounds – this is what I was told when I made inquiries – is that there is supposed to be in existence a certain letter which cannot be traced. I requested my office to contact Deputy Rabbitte to see if he could assist us in accelerating our inquiries and he was not in a position to give us much help . . . All the staff from the Attorney General's office available in the country have been interviewed about this matter and each and every one of them has said they have no knowledge whatsoever in this regard . . . No member of the staff who have been interviewed can assist in this regard. They say they have no knowledge of any such letter.'

Such was the level of speculation sweeping Leinster House that day, that the Catholic Primate, Cardinal Daly, was moved to dismiss as 'utterly absurd, untrue and a total fabrication' the rumours that he had made representations to the AG's office on behalf of Fr Smyth. 'I can't speak for everyone but I am quite certain that nothing is known to me about any approach whatsoever to anybody connected with this case,' he said, adding: 'It is incomprehensible to me how anybody could have invented such a story.'

The strength of Cardinal Daly's comments left little room for doubt and history has shown them to be entirely accurate. In *The Irish Times* the next day, one analyst wrote: 'Before the curtain fell on the day's events, a Fianna Fáil obfuscation machine was going into full trottle, feeding into or confirming, the most damaging fantasies of speeded up politicians. Pat Rabbitte talked of a document which would 'shake the state to its foundations' and from there with Fine Gael questions outstanding, it was only a hop, skip and a jump to linking Cardinal Daly and other Northern Bishops and politicians to the Smyth case. A formal statement from the Cardinal dismissing suggestions of religious interference as 'utterly absurd' laid the platform from which Mary Harney accused Fianna Fáil ministers of deliberately feeding the rumour machine.'

Despite all the rumours, what actually emerged later that same day in November 1994 was much more prosaic, although it was enough to bring down a government. Reynolds revealed that he had been told two days earlier by the new AG, Eoghan Fitzsimmons, that contrary to what the former AG Harry Whelehan had reported to the government, the Smyth case was not the first case to be considered under the provisions of the 1987 Extradition Act. This was critical because the argument that the Smyth case was the first such case had been given as one of the reasons for the delay in processing the case. Reynolds said Fitzsimmons' investigation had 'shown that in an extradition case in 1992, namely Duggan, executed by the former Attorney General, Mr. Whelehan, the section 50 provisions were considered.'

The Taoiseach added pointedly that he 'would have expected the most senior legal officer of this State to have known of the Duggan case of 1992 considering that he cleared the warrants for endorsement by the Garda Commissioner and that he would have made this information known to me and the Government. This information was not made known to me and the Government by the former Attorney General. Had my colleagues and I been aware of these facts last week, we would not have proposed or supported the nomination of Mr. Harry Whelehan as President of the High Court.' Reynolds added that he was 'informed that the former Attorney General [Whelehan] had forgotten about the Duggan case when he prepared and approved the report sent to me'. It should be pointed out that a later report into the affair found that Whelehan had not done anything wrong. Reynolds concluded that he now accepted that 'the reservations voiced by the Tánaiste [Dick Spring] are well founded and I regret the appointment of the former Attorney General as President of the High Court'. The problem for Labour was that this information had been given to Reynolds on Monday, the day before he stood up in the Dáil and stated that 'there is nothing to say he [Whelehan] is not as suitable for high office today as he was a few weeks ago'.

So the government fell but while most people today would struggle to recall the reasons for the collapse, Rabbitte's words about 'rocking the foundations of the state' – as it is now more commonly remembered – have never been forgotten. Fianna Fáil, in particular, has made more than one reference to them.

Just a couple of weeks later, Dick Roche raised Rabbitte's comments in the Seanad. 'That Deputy [Rabbitte] stood up and indicated to the Ceann Comhairle, with all the great theatrics he can bring to one of those magic moments in Dáil Éireann, that there existed a document in the Attorney General's office that would rock the very foundations of this State. The word went around Leinster House that there existed a letter or communication from a senior figure in the Catholic Church which contributed to the delay in the Smyth case.

'Deputy Rabbitte is of course known for making allegations which are later shown to be without any foundation. Mr. Justice

Hamilton rejected claim after claim by this public representative as being without foundation in the costly beef tribunal report. Deputy Rabbitte has not explained himself or apologised for those false claims. He should now have the honour and the integrity to come before the other House and either explain or produce the evidence to support the allegation he made that day. It is important as we are talking about integrity.'

It would prove a recurring theme in Fianna Fáil attacks on Rabbitte.

For example, in 2005, more than a decade after the comments were made, the Minister for Enterprise, Trade and Employment, Micheál Martin, reacted to criticism of his performance while Minister for Health in relation to the nursing homes issue. He said Rabbitte was prone to making outlandish statements and to hyperbole, which while colourful could also be wearing. 'He was the politician who famously declared to a stunned Dáil that information was to be revealed that would "rock the foundations of the State",' Martin said.

While Rabbitte unquestionably gaffed by going over-the-top in his comments, it did nothing to stop his rise in Irish politics. Within five years of his party merging with Labour, Rabbitte had become leader of the new party – his robust and colourful debating style was clearly a factor in his victory.

Honey, I VATted the Kids

John Bruton

THE BACKGROUND

It was 27 January, 1982 when the Fine Gael and Labour coalition government presented its first budget. The environment could not have been worse for that budget. The Irish economy was in the doldrums and the public finances were in a state of crisis, demanding tough restorative measures. To complicate matters, Garret FitzGerald's government needed the support of Independent TDs to survive in the Dáil, hardly a conducive setting in which to make the difficult decisions required.

THE GAFFE

John Bruton, the coalition's thrusting young Finance Minister, introduced a budget that the Independents felt they could not support. The coalition became the first government in the history of the state to collapse over a budget vote. To be fair to Bruton, he was trying to address the huge budget deficit and introduce some reality into the management of the public finances. But as *The Irish Times* editorial of two days later pointed out, failing to ensure they had the votes of the Independents on board was 'an idiotic error of judgement on the coalition's part'. For a minority government to go into a critical vote without first making sure it had the support required for its survival was unforgivably careless. The coalition paid a heavy price for that carelessness – they lost power.

The budget is best remembered for the decision to introduce VAT on children's clothing and footwear but the entirely logical and correct decision to reduce food subsidies may have proved just as damaging when it came to the Dáil vote.

By today's standards with giveaway budgets virtually the norm, it was a really severe budget, with increases in VAT, excise duties, income tax, postal and phone charges, capital taxes and social insurance contributions.

With 27% of all items zero rated, which was exceptionally high by European standards, it seemed sensible to expand the VAT base. Bruton took the decision to subject clothing and footwear – which previously had a zero rating – to the newly-increased VAT rate of 18%. He contended that when the exemption was introduced in 1975, more than half of clothing and footwear was produced domestically, whereas seven years on most was now imported. Furthermore, while clothing and footwear were obviously necessities, the zero rate covered 'everything from the most simple garments to the most expensive and ephemeral creations of fashion'. Bruton also said that he had considered the possibility of omitting children's clothing and footwear from the increase, as happened in the UK, but opted against it 'because I'm also aware of the major difficulties which it poses in practice and of the anomalies it has created'. He added that he considered it preferable to compensate parents directly through increased child benefit payments, which were quite generous given the limited resources of the exchequer.

Meanwhile, Bruton opted to cut the exchequer subsidy on butter and eliminate it on milk, maintaining the supports for bread, flour and margarine. The case for food subsidies helping the most marginalised in society was an extremely dubious one. Bruton noted that the subsidies were available to everyone and actually benefited the rich more as they were bigger buyers. He described the food subsidies as 'a somewhat wasteful mechanism for transferring resources'.

Regardless of whether it was a good decision or not, Independent TD Jim Kemmy, a lifelong socialist, had already told Fine Gael leader Garret FitzGerald that if food subsidies were tampered with in the budget, he would not support it. The government could ill-afford to lose his vote but his warnings went unheeded, until just minutes before the crucial vote. He said after that vote: 'they took me for granted. That was the mistake they made tonight'.

It was clear to some observers on budget day that the coalition was in serious trouble. Behind the scenes, Labour backbenchers were threatening to revolt over VAT on children's clothing. And just minutes before the first vote on the budget, FitzGerald approached Kemmy in the Dáil and asked for more time to amend the proposal in relation to VAT on children's clothing and footwear. However, Kemmy said that he had made up his mind and that the government had failed to deliver on his pre-budget demands. He had no alternative but to vote against the budget. According to *The Irish Times* the next day, the 'last gasp negotiations were brought to an abrupt end when Fianna Fáil deputies, crowded above them in the lobbies, theatrically shushed them. In the ensuing silence, [Fianna Fáil TD] Sean Moore walked down the steps and stood blatantly over them in order to put an end to their conversation.'

Kemmy voted with the opposition, as did Joe Sherlock of the Workers' Party and Independent TD Fianna Fáil TD Neil Blaney. Noel Browne voted with the government, but the coalition's fate was sealed when the remaining Independent Sean 'Dublin Bay' Loftus walked into the 'níl' lobby. The government lost the vote 82-81.

THE IMPACT

Although Fianna Fáil leader Charlie Haughey made himself available for consultation by the president about forming a government, the 22nd Dáil was dissolved and a general election was called for 18 February, 1982. At what was described as an 'emotional' Fine Gael parliamentary party meeting, FitzGerald and Bruton (the latter, in absentia) were given standing ovations, despite the government's defeat. However, Fine Gael TD Oliver J Flanagan got to the nub of the matter when he said the budget had been right in terms of the national good, but wrong politically. He quoted a saying from the time of the Napoleonic wars that warned that one had to survive first in order to win.

With the collapse of its government, Fine Gael had to face into an extremely difficult election campaign, given the unpopularity of its budget. However, they got immediate support in an editorial in *The Irish Times* which argued that 'if the citizens of this beleaguered little Republic placed any value on the virtues of tenacity and honesty and on their own future, they would return the coalition parties to government with a thumping majority'. The coalition had attempted to face up to the country's ills. It may have 'fumbled, mumbled and bumbled' from time to time but 'at least they made the effort'. Their defeat was not a reflection of their ability to lead but their political astuteness, it concluded.

However, the following day's editorial, describing the Dáil defeat as 'an idiotic error of judgement', chastised the coalition, noting that 'sometimes, especially in regard to Fine Gael, it seems as if their eyes are too fixedly aimed at the stars. Fianna Fáil are more aware of the clabber under foot.'

During the election campaign, the coalition undertook to exempt footwear and clothes for children under ten from VAT. Despite performing well in the difficult circumstances, it lost the election. Its seat losses were limited to just two. Fianna Fáil gained three seats, allowing Charlie Haughey to form a minority government, which would in turn collapse the following Autumn. By the end of 1983, Fine Gael and Labour were back in government with a good working majority. However, during its four years in power, it failed to get to grips with the crisis in the public finances in the way in which that first defeated budget threatened to do. It's hard to imagine that the experience of that defeat was not a factor in this failure. While Bruton, very much the golden boy of Fine Gael prior to his 1982 Budget, was damaged for a time by that same budget's defeat, he overcame the setback and became Taoiseach twelve years later.

Patter of Small Feet

Garret Fitzgerald

THE BACKGROUND

It was the night of 27 January, 1982 and Garret FitzGerald's Fine Gael-Labour coalition had just become the first government in the history of the State to fall on a budget vote (see Chapter 18). Today, their tough budget – an overdue attempt to tackle the disastrous public finances – is best remembered for the decision to introduce VAT on children's clothing and footwear, but it was the decision to reduce food subsidies that proved just as damaging when it came to the crucial Dáil vote. The minority government had carelessly gone into that vote without first making sure it had the requisite support.

It paid dearly for that carelessness. Independents Jim Kemmy and Sean Dublin Bay Loftus voted against the government and it lost by 82 votes to 81. Although defeated, Garret FitzGerald was not downhearted – quite the contrary. He wrote subsequently in his autobiography that on hearing the budget vote result he 'experienced a moment of total exhilaration: this was it'. His government was going to battle on a budget that 'we could defend with conviction and enthusiasm, both on social and financial grounds'. He claimed that his government's 'vigorous tackling of the financial crisis' and honesty in preparing its budget was in contrast to Fianna Fáil's 'appalling four year record of extravagance'. FitzGerald was also convinced that his government would have fallen anyway the following April when the 3.5% increase in social insurance contributions – shared equally between employers and employees – started to hit pay packets. The increased tax had hardly been noticed amid all the furore, but FitztGerald felt it was only a matter of time before the 'timebomb exploded'. He felt fighting an election in those circumstances could have seen Fine Gael lose all the gains it had made the previous June, whereas he now felt that, at worst, his government would lose a couple of seats.

THE GAFFE

At a press conference after the government had collapsed, FitzGerald was pressed on the VAT issue and asked if his government should have exempted children's wear from the new VAT rate of 18% on clothing and shoes. According to the following day's newspapers, the Taoiseach answered that this might have led to a situation where some women with small feet could have bought their shoes cheaper than their children who had larger feet.

THE IMPACT

It was a disastrous comment. Bad enough to be the first government to lose power on a budget vote, but the error was

compounded by what seemed to be a ludicrous explanation that only served to focus attention on the decision to impose VAT on children's clothes and footwear in the first place. It was not what the government parties needed facing into an already difficult election campaign. FitzGerald's explanation of what happened is extremely revealing. In his autobiography, he says that his 'buoyant mood betrayed me when I came to answer a question about why we had not exempted children's clothing and footwear from our extension of VAT to clothing generally'. It was an issue, he said, he had discussed with Department of Finance officials 'in the light of some early criticism' of this aspect of the budget. The problem, FitzGerald said, was 'I allowed my sense of humour to overcome my judgment, disclosing that I had been told by the officials that in Britain just such a distinction had given rise to intense public dissatisfaction because children with large feet had to buy adults' shoes, which carried the tax! The press, in a much more serious mood than I was, wrote this down solemnly as the actual reason which had led us to reject an exemption for children, whereas the financial considerations . . . had led us to conclude that we needed that money that would come from an undifferentiated tax on clothing and footwear.'

FitzGerald admitted that the comment was 'subsequently used against me mercilessly and although up to that point this question of children's clothing and footwear had not, I believe, been a significant factor in the defeat of the budget a short time earlier, the issue really took off from the moment I gave this answer – so much so, indeed that the February 1982 election is now firmly embedded in popular mythology as the election caused by our government's decision to impose VAT on children's shoes'.

No argument there, Garret. However, it should be pointed out that FitzGerald's initial feeling of euphoria was not entirely misplaced. His government did in fact only lose a couple of seats and, while Fianna Fáil returned to power, it was as a minority administration that collapsed the following November. By the end of the year, FitzGerald was back as Taoiseach with a working majority, despite – so to speak – having put a pair of size twos in it.

On a Small Island

Brian Lenihan

THE BACKGROUND

It was October 1987 and Ireland had not yet emerged from the depths of the worst economic downturn the country had endured since the 1950s. The country's finances were so bad in the mid 1980s that there was even talk of the International Monetary Fund being drafted in to try and help the situation. Unemployment was touching on 20% and tens of thousands of young Irish people opted to emigrate to the US, the UK or mainland Europe to find work. Overall, the mood was one of fatalistic pessimism in the country dubbed 'the sick man of Europe'.

However, there were small signs of the green shoots of recovery. Charlie Haughey had been returned to power in the general election of February 1987 and he and his Finance Minister Ray McSharry seemed determined to put some shape on the public finances by cutting sharply back on public spending. After ten years of fantasy politics, during which time all parties blatantly ignored sound economic principles and refused to face up to realities, the tough decisions were finally being made. The first national wage deal – the Programme for National Recovery – was agreed, marking the beginning of a new era of social partnership. However, a few more years of economic hardship lay ahead and it would be more than a decade before immigration replaced emigration as an economic reality in Ireland.

THE GAFFE

In September of 1987, Tanaiste and Foreign Affairs Minister Brian Lenihan visited the US for two weeks. While there, he did an interview with *Newsweek* magazine. In the interview, the affable and extremely intelligent Lenihan was asked if emigration was a defeat for Ireland. He replied: 'I don't look on the type of emigration we have today as being of the same category as the terrible emigration in the last century. What we have now is a very literate emigrant, who thinks nothing of coming to the United States and going back to Ireland and maybe onto Germany and back to Ireland again. The younger people in Ireland today are very much in that mode. And it's very refreshing to see it. If future legislation in the Congress will acknowledge the skills and capacities of Irish emigrants and grant legal status to allow entry to qualified jobs, we will have a mobile labour market stretching from the US to Ireland to the European Community where we can participate and contribute fully. It's not a defeat because the more they [Irish emigrants] hone their skills and their talents in another environment, the more they develop a work ethic in a country like Germany or the US, the better it can be applied to Ireland when they return'.

Then came what proved to be the really damaging part for the government. Asked what emigrants can offer Ireland, Lenihan responds: 'They should do what they have to do. The world is now one world and they can always return to Ireland with the skills they have developed. We regard them as part of a global generation of Irish people. We shouldn't be defeatist or pessimistic about it. We should be proud of it. After all, we can't all live on a small island.'

THE IMPACT

The interview was published the following month, headlined 'Exodus from a small island'. It wasn't long before the Irish media picked up on the story and, in the words of *The Irish Times*, the reaction was 'quick, indignant and angry'. Lenihan's comments proved a major embarrassment for the government. The last line in particular was thrown at Fianna Fáil as evidence that they had accepted that there was nothing that could be done about emigration and that they were not particularly worried about it.

The government reacted angrily to the way in which the Irish media reported the interview and to what it regarded as the unfair and damaging interpretation of it, i.e. that Lenihan was basically saying he was not worried about emigration. This 'could not be justified from any reasonable reading of the article,' a spokesman said. He was probably right but the spokesman was whistling against a gale. Opposition parties and immigrant lobby groups queued up to hammer Lenihan and the government. Fine Gael's foreign affairs spokesman Peter Barry said the comments were 'simply daft', adding: 'I am frankly shocked that he should say that the government is not worried that 40,000 Irish workers emigrate each year. While the government may not be worried, the parents of these young people are. These people have made great sacrifices to educate their children and it is madness for the benefits of this to be made available to another economy.'

The chairman of the Labour party, Michael Bell, called on the government to clarify its official position on the issue of emigration. 'If Mr Lenihan has been accurately reported, his comments represent a very significant and very disturbing u-turn in the government's attitude to the emigration of thousands of our young people every year.' And Pat McCartan of the Workers' Party said the 'extraordinary' comments 'indicated quite clearly that official government policy was now to encourage emigration'.

An Irish priest working with illegal immigrants in the US said the remarks confirmed the suspicions of those involved in welfare work that the government response was to export the problem of unemployment. The Immigration Reform Movement, which was involved in helping Irish immigrants in the US, described Lenihan's remarks as 'deeply disappointing'. It took issue with his use of the word 'refreshing', arguing: 'That's not the way it is. People don't want to leave Ireland. It's a matter of need.'

In an editorial headlined, 'Not another Brianism', *The Irish Times* said that Lenihan's 'off the cuff remarks and humorous asides have often cut through official pomposity and rhethorical blather to show the human face of politics and politicians'. But it added: 'This, however, was not just another Brianism. It was Mr

Haughey's most senior and trusted minister addressing an international audience on an issue which, for too many of our people, is far from trivial. Emigration, for those who do not choose to go, must always be considered, not an everyday option, but a last resort'.

The editorial was rightly scathing about Lenihan's comment that we couldn't all live on a small island – which must have been news to the inhabitants of the Netherlands who have a population five times greater than Ireland's living in around half the area. 'This is the most sparsely populated country in western Europe. That it should be so is a sad reflection on the way we have conducted our affairs since achieving independence. By suggesting that it is likely to continue to be so, the Tanaiste inadvertently casts doubt on the high expectation of the Programme for National Recovery. The damage done is not irreparable, but it will take the best efforts of the government – and the social partners, who are committed to the programme – to prove that Mr Lenihan was not once more letting the cat out of the official bag,' the editorial warned.

Lenihan, a very popular politician, was renowned for always putting a positive spin on things. His catchphrase was 'no problem' and the interview with *Newsweek* was probably simply a case of him trying to put the country's best face forward to an international audience and to avoid washing our dirty laundry in public. Responding to the opposition criticism at the height of the controversy, Lenihan told journalists that the government was 'very concerned, but not necessarily worried' about emigration. 'Being worried implies you are worried and doing nothing. I and the government will do everything that is possible to do something positive about the problem.'

One of the few people to come out and back Lenihan was the

legendary Fine Gael TD John Kelly. In his usual colourful style, Kelly said that the Minister might not be too pleased at being congratulated because 'after 25 years of reckless spoofing, [he] has at last decided to tell the bare truth as he sees it'. And he joked that it was unlikely that the rest of Fianna Fáil would follow Lenihan's 'reforming example' after seeing him (Lenihan) 'assailed on all sides for his completely sensible remarks on emigration'.

Kelly argued that Lenihan was 'obviously right' in what he said. Instead of warning people about the realities of a population explosion occurring alongside a recession in the world economy, politicians on all sides had pretended there were tens of thousands of jobs just waiting to be created. 'Mr Lenihan has at last thrown up the windows and opened the doors of the smoke filled rooms of which, in popular folklore, he is the archetypal occupant. Instead of shouting him down, his critics would be better occupied drawing some sensible implications, above all in the field of education policy, from the plain facts he has opened to public view.'

As we now know there was, and is, room for all of us on the island. Since the difficult 1980s, the population of the country has grown dramatically and from a position of 40,000 people leaving a year, Ireland has become the country with the highest per capita rate of immigration in the world. Probably no politician would have been more proud of that fact than Lenihan himself, who sadly died at just 64 in 1995 – just as the Celtic Tiger was beginning its roar.

Nice to 'No' You

Eamon Ó Cuív

THE BACKGROUND

A referendum on the Nice Treaty was held in June 2001. This treaty was designed to overhaul the EU institutions in advance of the enlargement of the Union. Despite the backing of the Fianna Fáil/Progressive Democrats coalition government and the main opposition parties, the referendum was defeated – a major embarrassment for the political establishment.

THE GAFFE

Eamon Ó Cuív, Fianna Fáil TD and Minister of State for Agriculture and Rural Development, declared in an interview on TG4 that he had actually voted against the Nice Treaty, in contrast to the stated policy of the government in which he was a Minister.

THE IMPACT

There was ill-disguised fury in government circles at Ó Cuív's revelation. Opposition parties called for him to resign if he disagreed with government policy on Nice.

Ó Cuív said in the TG4 interview that he objected to EU bureaucrats getting more power and later claimed: 'A citizen has the right to vote whatever way he, or she, likes. A minister is also a citizen, besides being a minister.'

Defending his decision to reveal his 'no' vote, he told one newspaper: 'I suppose that I am one of those people who tells things as they are, who doesn't hide their view. Most people would have known what my view was anyway. If people want to attack me, fine. It is part of politics to get attacked.'

He also said he had adhered to the government's campaign on Nice 'as I was obliged to do, and as I accept that I am obliged to do'.

Despite the controversy, Citizen Ó Cuív's stance had no negative impact on his career. His views are believed to have gone down well in his constituency of Galway West, where there is a view that small farmers and fishermen are not fully convinced of the benefits of EU membership. He topped the poll in the 2002 general election the following year.

Rather than being demoted for his stand, a year later the Taoiseach actually promoted him to a full cabinet ministry after the general election – 'Nice' work if you can get it.

In the second Nice referendum, Ó Cuív supported the government line – a decision described by one constituency rival, Niall O Brolcháin of the Greens, as a 'good old fashioned Fianna Fáil U-turn'. Ó Cuív denied that his decision to support the Treaty in the second referendum was associated in any way with the Taoiseach's decision to promote him to cabinet.

Crap, Total Crap

Albert Reynolds

THE BACKGROUND

It was October 1992 and what had been described as a 'temporary little arrangement' between Fianna Fáil and the Progressive Democrats was falling apart. Charlie Haughey and Des O'Malley had surprised everybody by effectively coalescing together, despite their old enmity. However, it was quickly clear that relations between O'Malley and Haughey's successor Albert Reynolds were exceptionally strained. Their conflicting positions at the Beef Tribunal, which was running at the time in Dublin Castle, was the main problem.

During the summer, on his fifth day in the witness box, O'Malley said that decisions taken by Albert Reynolds on the beef export credit insurance scheme had been 'wrong . . . grossly unwise, reckless and foolish'. While O'Malley had not questioned Reynolds' integrity, and the remarks related to events of five years earlier, they were still remarkable comments for a de-facto Tanaiste (unlike Mary Harney in the later FF/PD coalition, O'Malley never held the position of Tanaiste) to make

about a Taoiseach. The remarks were not sufficient to bring down the government but it was clear that it would be only a matter of time before open warfare would break out between the two government parties. Relations were further strained by a row over a suggestion in the Culliton Report that the Industrial Development Agency (IDA) should be split into separate agencies – one to support indigenous industry, the other to attract inward investment. O'Malley supported the idea but Reynolds opposed it. Next Reynolds stopped Mary Harney, then a junior minister, from representing the PDs at North-South talks in Dublin Castle. Harney had been nominated by O'Malley but Reynolds vetoed her on the grounds that she was not a member of the cabinet. But all these secondary issues paled into insignificance when Reynolds, giving evidence to the Beef Tribunal, described O'Malley's evidence as 'reckless, irresponsible and dishonest'.

Suddenly, the country was on the verge of an election. In a move towards compromise, Reynolds conducted an exclusive interview with then political editor of the *Sunday Tribune* Gerry Barry, in which he stated his door was always open to the PD ministers. Sean Duignan, Reynolds' government press secretary, recalls in his book *One Spin on the Merry-Go-Round* that at the end of the interview, Barry asked Reynolds about allegations that he never spoke to O'Malley outside of cabinet. Although he gave an initial non-committal response, Reynolds returned to the subject as Barry was leaving. 'You want to know what I think of that – it's crap, pure crap'. According to Duignan, 'Gerry chuckled at the word "crap", appreciatively repeating it after Reynolds, and this elicited the following: "I mean that – for the record – it's crap, total crap".' The *Sunday Tribune* prominently ran the 'crap' reference, but there was no reaction to it from other newspapers.

THE GAFFE

The day that the *Sunday Tribune* ran the interview, Reynolds was doorstepped arriving at a function. He once again, as Duignan recalls in his book, 'pronounced the O'Malley arguments "crap, total crap". This time, however, he was on camera, on "mike" and on prime time national news. On screen, it looked and sounded wrong.'

THE IMPACT

The 'crap' hit the fan. Looking back, while the words used seem particularly mild, the comments were a PR disaster for Reynolds, with many people, particularly older voters, regarding the language as unstatesmanlike. The timing was particularly unfortunate. In normal circumstances, people would have quickly forgotten the comments, politics would have moved on. But within days, Reynolds and Fianna Fáil were in the thick of a general election campaign as the PDs pulled out of government. In *One Spin on the Merry-Go-Round*, Duignan said that he had figured that the *Sunday Tribune* report with the 'crap' line might raise eyebrows, but he hoped it would pass off because most readers would assume the Taoiseach had not meant it for publication. 'What had not occurred to me, however, was that the Taoiseach might actually relish the phrase, figure that it was within bounds and decide to recycle it'.

Duignan said the remarks on television 'cost Reynolds dearly during the upcoming election campaign, primarily because it perfectly fitted the grotesque Reynolds caricature being drawn by his opponents, that of a coarse and boorish man'.

One commentator wrote in the *Irish Independent*, a few days after the comment was made, that the 'promotion of O'Malley's integrity will be helped, initially anyway, by the Taoiseach's latest linguistic gaffe – his crass resort to the use of the word 'crap. The 'c' word will be put by the PDs, into the verbal ring in all 41 constituencies in contention'. Another columnist in the same paper wrote that Reynolds' 'comment has offended people who like their leaders to speak in loftier language'. Conor Cruise O'Brien wrote that Reynolds was the 'first Taoiseach ever to use the word 'crap' in public. This is not a niche in history that any sensible politician would covet. It is clear that his language offended many of our people. In two RTÉ phone-ins, listeners protested against a Taoiseach setting a bad example to the young. This is hardly the way to set about winning an overall majority for Fianna Fáil.'

The election proved a disaster for Reynolds and Fianna Fáil, with people blaming them for the collapse of the government. Far from winning an overall majority, Fianna Fáil lost nine seats, while the PDs more than doubled their seat numbers. However, while it was a 'crap' result for his party, the outcome wasn't 'total crap' for Reynolds, who managed to stay on as Taoiseach by doing a deal with the big winners of the election – the Labour Party – to form a new coalition government.

The First Social Martyrs

Ernest Blythe

THE BACKGROUND

In 1924, with the War of Independence and the Civil War over, Cumann na nGaedheal set about the more mundane business of running the fledgling Free State. Although it contained many talented figures, it was an extremely socially conservative government and none more so than its Minister for Finance, Ernest Blythe. An Irish language enthusiast, he was heavily involved in the activities of the Irish Volunteers and spent Easter 1916 in prison – one of the many times he was arrested under the Defence of the Realm Act. He was just 34 years old when he was appointed Minister for Finance, a position he retained until 1932.

Historian Joe Lee described Blythe as having a 'strong personality of narrow perspective' and of being a 'Christian brothers' boy par excellence – except that he was an Ulster Protestant!' The new government did not inherit an easy situation. The domestic economy was struggling and there was a high financial price to pay for the War of Independence and the Civil War. The government engaged in what Lee described as 'rigorous retrenchment'. Blythe, he noted, had a financial policy but 'virtually no economic policy beyond the act of faith that prosperity would follow from fiscal rectitude'. The new government set about balancing the books at all costs. Cumann na nGaedheal actually reduced overall government spending from £42 million in 1923/24 to £32 million in 1924/25 and £24 million in 1926/27 – a feat that seems incredible in today's Ireland, in which government spending increases by 7% or 8% each year. In tandem with its policy of tight controls on spending, the government set about reducing taxation. In 1924, it was able to reduce income tax from five shillings to just three shillings – 6d lower than England. As well as proving to doubters across the Irish Sea that the Irish could govern responsibly, the government cut income tax in a misguided effort to attract capital to Ireland (unfortunately, with relatively high levels of savings at the time, a shortage of capital was not a problem for the State).

THE GAFFE

In 1924, in order to ensure the books were balanced, Blythe took the extreme decision to cut the old age pension and the pensions for the blind by 10%. A shilling was cut off the old age pension, reducing it from ten shillings (roughly 63 cents) to nine shillings (roughly 57 cents) a week. The result of his drastic action reduced government expenditure on these pensions from £3.18 million in 1924 to £2.54 million three years later.

THE IMPACT

Blythe's measure might have balanced the books but, not surprisingly, there was widespread criticism of the decision, which was used as a stick to beat the government with for many years afterwards. For example, four years later, in 1928, Labour TD Daniel Morrissey – who ironically went on to become a Cumann na nGaedheal minister – described the move in the Dáil as the 'most shameful act ever passed in this house'. The government had made old people 'the first social martyrs of Irish liberty' with a budget measure that was 'universally condemned and regarded as a stain upon the state,' Morrissey said. He was far from alone in his views.

Blythe, however, was unbowed by the sharp criticism. He strongly defended his decision and attempted to turn the tables on some of his critics by insisting that the destruction caused by the Civil War 'can be taken to be solely responsible for this particular cut'. The compensation charges, army charges and general cost of the destruction left the government 'faced with a deficit so great that it cannot be met without much more drastic measures'. The government simply had to 'put the house in order'. Its actions now would save pensioners from a much more damaging state of affairs where the government would be forced to 'greatly' raise taxation. Those people who argued against the move were speaking from the depths of emotions, he said.

While the tough decisions on spending left the government free to cut taxes, which played well with Cumann na nGaedheal's more prosperous core support, there seems to be little doubt that, in the long term, the cut in the pensions – along with other austere measures such as cutting pay for teachers and policemen

– damaged the party politically. These tough budgetary measures allowed a caricature of the party as being 'out of touch' to build up. In 1926, Eamon de Valera founded Fianna Fáil and the new party proved hugely adept at populist politics in a way in which Cumann na nGaedheal – and later Fine Gael – was never capable. Historian John A Murphy said that first government 'had little savvy in anticipating or gauging popular reaction to its often severe measures. Its political opponents made sure that 'cutting a shilling off the old age pension' in 1924 would enter and remain in the negative folklore.' The cut in the pensions and a more legitimate – but still unpopular – decision to tighten up procedures for processing pension claims, seems to have particularly affected the party in the west of the country, where one in four families had a pensioner.

Blythe continued in his role as one of the country's most powerful politicians – adding Post and Telegraphs to his responsibilities as Finance Minister and also becoming Vice President of the Executive Council (effectively the job of Tanaiste today) until the early 1930s. Fianna Fáil inevitably won power in 1932. True to its populist instincts, it quickly set about increasing the pension. The following year, Blythe lost his Dáil seat in Monaghan, with many commentators believing that the unpopularity of his austere financial measures were the main factor in this defeat. He served for a time in the Seanad and was a senior figure in the Blueshirts, but he became an increasingly isolated figure in the new Fine Gael once the party got rid of Eoin O'Duffy. He served between 1941 and 1967 as managing director of the Abbey Theatre, where his commercial focus was not always welcomed by the theatre's actors – a case of art imitating life?

Here Comes the Judge

Charlie McCreevy

THE BACKGROUND

In 1999, a major controversy, which will be forever remembered as the Sheedy Affair, resulted in the unprecedented resignations of a Supreme Court Judge, a High Court Judge and a senior judicial officer. That controversy centred on the early release from jail of a young Dublin architect, Philip Sheedy, who had received a four year sentence for dangerous driving causing death. Just over a year into his sentence, Circuit Court Judge Cyril Kelly, sitting at Dublin Circuit Criminal Court, suspended the balance of Sheedy's sentence. Kelly was not the original sentencing judge.

It later emerged that Supreme Court Judge Hugh O'Flaherty had asked the county registrar if the case could be put back into the list for hearing. O'Flaherty – who had previously been talked about as a potential candidate for the prestigious position of chief justice – and Kelly were effectively forced, in the resulting furore, into resignation by the government. A report emerged in the *Sunday Tribune* shortly afterwards that in 1998

Taoiseach Bertie Ahern had made representations on Sheedy's behalf, asking about the possibility of regular day release for Sheedy. While Ahern informed Tanaiste Mary Harney of this before the story broke, a major row developed between the two coalition partners (Fianna Fáil and the Progressive Democrats) when the Taoiseach publicly dismissed Harney's concerns and denied that she had asked him to make a statement to the Dáil on the issue. Harney was furious, refused to attend a cabinet meeting and it looked for a short time like the government would fall. The crisis passed when Ahern agreed to go into the Dáil and deal with the issue. However, the Sheedy Affair had not gone away.

THE GAFFE

Fast forward 13 months to 2000. The controversy that prompted the resignation of two judges had faded from public memory. On the 19 May, 2000, Finance Minister Charlie McCreevy announced that the government had nominated O'Flaherty for the IR£147,000 per annum vice presidency of the European Investment Bank (EIB).

THE IMPACT

All hell broke loose and there was a massive public backlash against the decision. If the government had been willing to take impeachment proceedings against O'Flaherty the previous year, why was he now being rewarded with such a plum job in Europe? The political fallout was enormous. The opposition accused the government of a 'most scandalous act of political patronage and nepotism' and engaging in 'stroke' politics. The whole Sheedy Affair was re-opened. It emerged that agreement for the nomination was secured through a ring-around of senior ministers, rather than through discussions at cabinet.

McCreevy wasn't the only one in the line of fire. The PDs, who had traditionally taken on the watchdog role in government, were the focus of much criticism. A spokesman for Mary Harney confirmed she was consulted and raised no objection. However, the decision went down very badly with the PD foot soldiers. Within days, Harney told a PD parliamentary party meeting she was wrong not to consult with them before agreeing to the nomination. There was also extreme irritation within Fianna Fáil over the decision, as TDs and senators got it in the neck from their constituents.

At first the government hung tough. The message seemed to be: O'Flaherty will receive his EU nomination come hell or high water. However, unusually the issue didn't die away. Public attention and the accusations of arrogance refused to fade away in what proved to be a long hot summer for the government. In a by-election in Tipperary South, Fianna Fáil's vote collapsed and TDs weren't long about apportioning blame.

There was more embarrassment for the government when in June, the Finance Minister was ordered not to proceed with the nomination pending a judicial review of proceedings brought by Denis Riordan, a lecturer at the Limerick Institute of Technology. Although the High Court ruled that the nomination could proceed, Riordan appealed the decision to the Supreme Court.

Tensions in government rose when the Taoiseach in a radio interview said it would be 'helpful' if O'Flaherty explained his role in the Sheedy case. Reports said that the Tanaiste was furious at the Taoiseach's apparent move to distance himself from the nomination thus effectively passing the buck to McCreevy and the PDs.

O'Flaherty himself entered the debate by giving interviews to TV3 and Today FM. He said that the Sheedy case had seemed to him 'a matter of simple justice'.

The government had to face a no-confidence motion on the issue in the Dáil. While it won the vote, it agreed in the Supreme Court not to take further steps on the appointment, pending a ruling on Riordan's appeal. Significantly, it then emerged that the EIB was prepared to consider other nominees.

At the end of July 2000, the Supreme Court ruled against Riordan, allowing the nomination to proceed. However, by August, it was clear that the EIB did not see O'Flaherty's nomination as straightforward – this would prove critical.

It emerged that Brussels was not immune to events in Ireland. O'Flaherty did not have the support of a majority of the 25 EIB directors, which he needed in order to have his nomination ratified. It was reported that in spite of political pressure and intensive lobbying, O'Flaherty had secured only six of the necessary 13 votes.

The writing was on the wall and at the end of August, O'Flaherty, in a dignified letter, requested to have his name withdrawn. McCreevy said he was 'disappointed at the decision' but understood why O'Flaherty had taken this course. The Tanaiste said it was the right thing to do. The controversy which had arisen was regrettable 'and it would not have been desirable to have had a divisive vote at the EIB'.

A senior civil servant, Michael Tutty, was appointed to the position instead by the government.

Fine Gael reacted to news of O'Flaherty's withdrawal by repeating its call for a sworn public inquiry into the Sheedy

Affair. Its finance spokesman Michael Noonan said McCreevy, having staked his political judgment on the nomination of O'Flaherty, should resign.

For his part, McCreevy acknowledged that the nomination had been 'a mistake' and the government had been 'damaged' by the affair.

'The controversy over the nomination of Mr Hugh O'Flaherty has been damaging to a lot of people. It has been very traumatic and it has generated an awful lot of headlines. Not all decisions that governments make are universally popular. We intend to move on. It was a mistake.'

McCreevy insisted that the idea of nominating O'Flaherty came from him alone. He specifically denied that the Taoiseach had come up with the idea, that O'Flaherty had sought the job or that there had been any promise given to O'Flaherty of a job when he resigned as a Supreme Court Judge the previous year.

The Finance Minister said he understood that journalists would have difficulty in believing he had initiated the nomination, given that he didn't know Hugh O'Flaherty. 'The one thing about this that no one can understand is how he got the job in the first place. Sure it's Ireland, it must have been lobbying, it must have been part of something. It wasn't. It wasn't part of any deal. It wasn't part of anything else. I just nominated him for reasons I have outlined here today, I outlined the same reasons in the Dáil and many other places.'

McCreevy said that 'an awful lot of people' would have felt that O'Flaherty 'paid a particularly heavy price for what the Chief Justice described at the time as actions motivated on a humanitarian basis'.

'I think that the Taoiseach and others have said that Mr O'Flaherty was in the running to be Chief Justice of the country.

That's on a par of status with the President of the country and the Taoiseach of the country, and Mr O'Flaherty was denied that opportunity on account of the events of 1999.

'I thought Mr O'Flaherty would be a suitable candidate for Ireland to put forward to this European job. I discussed this with the Taoiseach and the Tanaiste initially, we talked about it. We hadn't a big debate about it, but we discussed that he was a very suitable person. After that I decided to have discussions with my Cabinet colleagues as well.'

For a short time, it appeared that the damage to the government could be enormous – with the kind of impact on its popularity that Paddy Donegan's 'Thundering Disgrace' comments had on the Fine Gael/Labour government in the mid 1970s (see Chapter 43). An opinion poll carried out that September found that almost four out of five voters believed the affair damaged the government. Just six per cent said it did not. Privately, Fianna Fáil TDs expressed fears that it would cost the party seats at the next general election.

However, the most surprising thing about the whole affair was how short-lived the damage proved to be for the government, particularly given the perception of huge public anger over O'Flaherty's nomination.

Far from losing seats, within two years, Fianna Fáil and the PDs became the first government in over thirty years to be re-elected, buoyed by a succession of giveaway McCreevy budgets. Fianna Fáil came within a few hundred votes of an overall majority; the PDs doubled its seat total and the main opposition party was annihilated.

But the whole controversy must have been particularly bruising for Hugh O'Flaherty and his family. As Charlie McCreevy put it, by offering him the job, 'I brought an awful lot of trouble on Mr O'Flaherty and his wife and family.'

Short Memories

Mary Harney

THE BACKGROUND

It was June 2000 and Mary Harney was enduring probably the worst month of her long and distinguished political career. Judge Kevin Haugh had placed an indefinite stay on the trial of her old foe Charlie Haughey, who had been charged with obstructing the McCracken Tribunal. Harney's comments to the media that Haughey should be jailed were cited as a major reason for the postponement. Judge Haugh's decision prompted calls for Harney's resignation (see Chapter 5).

But the Tanaiste's problems didn't end there. She and the Progressive Democrats were getting it in the neck for failing to veto Charlie McCreevy's controversial nomination of Hugh O'Flaherty to the European Investment Bank (EIB) (see Chapter 24). O'Flaherty had been forced to resign as a Supreme Court judge in 1999 for his role in the Sheedy Affair. The public was outraged at the decision to then nominate him to a IR£147,000 per annum job as vice president of the EIB. The PDs took most of the flak probably because they appeared to have failed in their traditional self-appointed role as watchdog of the government. The watchdog failed to bark, never mind show its teeth, its critics claimed.

THE GAFFE

During a trip to Galway at the height of the controversy, Harney defended the decision to appoint O'Flaherty. It had been made in good faith and endorsed by the government. She said she believed it was a Christian thing to give a person a second chance – so far, so ok. But then the Tanaiste went on to say there were 'far more important issues in the country and I would predict that in three or four months time, it will not be remembered. The public's memory can often be short term.'

THE IMPACT

Harney got hammered for the remarks which would be used against her by opponents for years afterwards. Her comment about the electorate having short memories was seized upon as evidence that she and her government colleagues were out-of-touch and did not comprehend the enormous anger felt by the public over the decision to nominate O'Flaherty.

One commentator in the *Irish Independent* wrote that 'far from being an issue swiftly forgotten by the public – which is Mary Harney's mistaken interpretation of the impact of the O'Flaherty affair on the standing of the government – the event has touched a public nerve centre in a peculiarly sensitive way'.

Her close colleague, Junior Minister Liz O'Donnell, admitted that, 'it is not true that people will forget this. It has offended people's sense of justice. It wasn't just an unpopular decision, but a wrong decision.'

The PDs were reeling over the controversy. Harney's personal approval rating dipped by a massive 13 points to 46% in an opinion poll that month, June 2000, making it her lowest rating since becoming leader of the PDs.

To make matters worse for Harney, less than a fortnight later, she claimed that she never said people would not remember the appointment of O'Flaherty in three months. 'If I was accurately reported, I might get fair play. The last few weeks have been very difficult politically but I want to get on with tackling inflation and reforming company law'. Within an hour, RTÉ was playing a tape containing the inflammatory words.

The irony of the whole matter is that Harney was actually largely correct in making the point that the 'public's memory can often be short term'. Consider the facts with the benefit of hindsight. The government seemed to be on the verge of collapse during the summer of 2000 as the public's outrage reached boiling point. Voters, we were continually told, would be 'waiting in the long grass' for the government parties at the next election. But once O'Flaherty requested the withdrawal of his name from the nomination, the heat went out of the story virtually straight away.

The government's ratings picked up and within a few short months, John Bruton had been forced out as leader of Fine Gael because of that party's continued failure to make inroads into the government's lead in the opinion polls. In 2002, two years after Harney made the infamous comments, the FF/PD coalition – on the back of an unprecedented economic boom – became the first government in over thirty years to be re-elected. The opposition parties had been routed. Harney was right in what she said. The electorate does forget quickly. Her mistake was in expressing that opinion into a microphone.

Kebabs Lenihan

Conor Lenihan

THE BACKGROUND

In the first half of 2005, Socialist Party TD Joe Higgins had successfully campaigned on behalf of immigrant Turkish construction workers, who were working on state projects in Ireland for Turkish multinational GAMA Construction. In February of that year, Higgins said in the Dáil that the workers were paid €3 an hour, basic pay. He described it as a 'modern version of bonded labour'.

THE GAFFE

During Leaders' Questions in the Dáil on 18 May, 2006, Higgins rounded on Fianna Fáil deputies for their silence over the future ownership of Aer Lingus, labelling it the 'silence of the lambs'. It was all too much for Junior Minister Conor Lenihan who interjected, heckling that 'deputy Higgins should stick with the kebabs'.

THE IMPACT

Higgins immediately reacted in the Dáil, stating that 'the snide comment from behind the Taoiseach that I should stick with the kebabs, referrring to my fight against the exploitation of GAMA workers, ill behoves the Minister of State at the Department of Foreign Affairs, who has responsibility for overseas development'.

Speaking on radio later, Higgins turned up the temperature saying Lenihan should resign his ministry if he was referring to Turkish GAMA workers as kebabs. One GAMA worker was quoted as saying that the remark was a 'big insult' and he and his colleagues were 'very offended' by it.

A national newspaper ran a cartoon on its front page depicting Lenihan roasting on a spit and it must have felt like that for the hapless Minister.

Lenihan – who acquired the nickname 'Crazyhorse' while working as a broadcast journalist – bolted back into the Dáil chamber later that day to say he regretted the remarks, adding that 'I apologise sincerely if any offence was taken from the remarks'. A few hours later, his senior Minister at the Department of Foreign Affairs, Dermot Ahern, said he did not think Lenihan needed to re-evaluate his position. Ahern said Lenihan was contrite and as far as he was concerned that was the end of the matter.

But it wasn't – at least not for a few more days. The following week an editorial in *The Irish Times* accused Lenihan of making 'an entirely gratuitous remark belittling Turkish people as "kebabs".' The remark, the editorial said, was intended to imply that 'the welfare of Turkish workers in Ireland was a piddling subject fit for the likes of Joe Higgins, who should therefore leave the big boys to debate important issues'.

Noting the 'if' in his apology, the newspaper accused Lenihan of using 'weasel words'. Claiming that had it happened in another country there would have been a resignation, it concluded: 'We on the other hand are apparently not too bothered about offensive jibes – so long as they're not directed at the Irish. And that's a real slur on Ireland.'

Despite the furore, there was never any likelihood of Lenihan having to resign. While the remarks were regarded as stupid and offensive, most people in the Dáil accepted that, in the words of one commentator, Lenihan had 'opened his mouth before engaging his brain' and had not meant it as a slur against Turkish workers.

The Taoiseach and the Prince

John Bruton

THE BACKGROUND

On 31 May, 1995, Prince Charles made a two-day visit to Ireland. The visit at the time was seen as hugely historic, although in retrospect it will hardly warrant a footnote when the ultimate history of the peace process in Northern Ireland is finally recorded. Charles was the first member of the British royal family to be hosted by a government of the Irish State and it had been 84 years since a Prince of Wales had visited Ireland. Although there were protests and a few eggs were thrown, the visit was generally well received. To mark the occasion, a banquet was held in Dublin Castle, once seen as the foremost symbol of British rule in Ireland. As Taoiseach, it fell to John Bruton to play host – a role he took on with no little enthusiasm.

THE GAFFE

A clearly emotional Bruton went over the top in the phraseology he used to describe the visit. Departing from his script at times, the Taoiseach told Charles that his 'courage and initiative in coming here has done more to sweep away the legacy of fear and suspicion which has lain between our two peoples than any other event in my lifetime'. The prince's visit, he added, was 'doing more than any symbolic event in recent years to exorcise the past'. Certain memories had 'lain between our two peoples like a sword,' the Taoiseach said.

Those present to this day swear that Bruton also described the visit as 'the happiest day of my life', but while the quote may have entered folklore, it did not appear in the national newspapers in the days following the visit.

THE IMPACT

Little enough at first. *The Irish Times* editorial the next day said Bruton had 'found the right balance'. It fell to the London-based *Guardian* newspaper to sum up the feelings of many outside observers. It was tolerable, the newspaper's editorial said, for British public figures to be 'needlessly sycophantic' towards the royal family but it expressed concern about the international spread of sycophancy amid evidence that 'the Irish of all people had caught the hyperbole bug'. Referring to Bruton's line about the visit doing more 'than any other event in my lifetime', the editorial thundered: 'Mr Bruton is 48 and otherwise in splendid command of his senses, but can he really believe that the Prince's visit justifies such an extravagantly non-sensical attitude'. If anything, it concluded, the visit was 'a mark of the dull normality which is slowly coming to characterise relations between the two islands'. *The Times* of London did not single out Bruton but referred to 'embarrassingly enthusiastic speeches of greeting'.

Apart from a bit of teasing, however, Bruton's overenthusiastic reaction to the visit did not do him any harm politically or electorally. And to be fair to the Taoiseach, he was genuinely moved and excited by a visit that would have seemed impossible even a couple of years earlier. He was not the only one. There was blanket coverage of the event in all the media and given the country's status as a republic, there was – in the words of one media commentator at the time – 'one helluva royal love in'. Perhaps the most significant moment of the entire trip was in Dublin Castle when Bruton proposed a toast to the Queen which was impeccably observed by all present. A toast to the Queen of the United Kingdom of Great Britain and Northern Ireland, with her son and heir in the room, at a time when articles two and three of the constitution were still in place? Perhaps it was a once-in-a-lifetime event after all.

Lumumba-Jumba

Enda Kenny

THE BACKGROUND

After the general election of 2002, Enda Kenny was elected leader of a decimated Fine Gael. The task facing him was enormous. The party had lost 23 seats in the election and many commentators were openly predicting its demise. Kenny's job was to revive a party that had not won a general election in two decades.

THE GAFFE

Only a short time into his new position, Kenny almost committed political hari-kari. At a farewell drinks party in September for Fine Gael's departing press director – held in the basement bar of Buswell's Hotel – Kenny used the word 'nigger' in his speech to TDs, senators, party colleagues and journalists.

It had been a very difficult day for Kenny because an old

friend, former Tipperary TD David Molony, had died suddenly. Speaking about his late friend, Kenny recounted an anecdote about the time he, Molony and Senator Maurice Manning were in a bar in Portugal. They noticed that a cocktail on the menu was called a Lumumba. The three politicians speculated that this drink might be named after the African nationalist leader, Patrice Lumumba, the Congo's first democratically elected leader who was assassinated in 1961.

Kenny recalled that Manning asked the Moroccan barman about the origin of the drink's name, only to be told it was named after 'some nigger who died dans la guerre [in the war]'. The Fine Gael leader also referred to the barman's 'shiny teeth' and on three occasions said that he did not want to see the story in the newspapers. However, his warnings went unheeded and his comments were splashed across a leading Sunday newspaper that weekend.

THE IMPACT

The story proved a massive embarrassment for a man who was putting himself forward as the country's next Taoiseach. The Irish Refugee Council, the Irish Council for Civil Liberties and the Labour Party all condemned the use of the word 'nigger'. Peter O'Mahony of the Irish Refugee Council said that while it was difficult to 'put this kind of thing into context, I can think of no situation where that type of language and where the use of the word 'nigger' is appropriate. It was at best an ill-judged use of language. I think it is easy to be overly politically correct when you are involved in discussions on race but I don't think that this is an issue of what is politically correct or not. Language like this cheapens the debate and we have to find out why a particular senior politician felt it necessary to use that anecdote. ███ if we assume he was relating some other person's █████ anguage, it is absolutely wrong and entirely inappropriate to use that word.'

Kenny immediately apologised for the remark. In a statement, he said: 'I used a word I should never have used and I apologise unreservedly for it. Some of the people, in whose company I used this, have gone to great lengths to explain the word was used in recounting a true incident in the past. However, the fact is that I used the word, and no context excuses it. I failed to exemplify my own standards and the standards of a party absolutely committed to diversity. I am sorry.'

One Fine Gael figure, quoted in *The Irish Times*, who was present at Kenny's speech, stressed that the laugh wasn't supposed to be provoked by the word 'nigger'. 'The laugh was supposed to come from the picture of these three white guys in a bar in Portugal laughing at a Moroccan guy who dismissed a famous African leader as a 'nigger', an epithet none of the white guys would dream of using.'

While this was in all likelihood the case and while nobody believed Kenny was racist in any way, it raised serious question marks at the time about the Fine Gael leader's judgement that he would tell such a risqué story in front of journalists.

Interest in the story quickly dropped off, but it did take Kenny some time to recover from the setback. However, any damage to him did not prove to be long lasting. He defied his critics who had scoffed at his promise to electrify Fine Gael. In the local and European elections of 2004, Kenny led Fine Gael to a stunning performance winning more European seats than Fianna Fáil.

Have I Got News For You!

Phil Hogan

THE BACKGROUND

In February 1995, the newly formed Rainbow coalition of Fine Gael, Labour and Democratic Left was preparing to deliver its first budget. The government was formed out of the extraordinary collapse of the Fianna Fáil/Labour coalition the previous November. New Taoiseach John Bruton, understandably thrilled at his unexpected good fortune, gave an immediate hostage to fortune by saying that the new government must always be seen as operating behind a pane of glass.

However, two months into office, it was clear that the three government parties still viewed each other as competitors rather than partners. There was a virtual barrage of pre-budget leaks by all three parties, each championing what their own ministers had achieved, making a joke of the supposed confidentiality of the budgetary process.

THE GAFFE

At 12.15pm on budget day, a fax was sent to the newsdesks of both the *Evening Press* and the *Evening Herald*. Bearing the name of the Junior Minister at the Department of Finance, Phil Hogan, and his political advisor, the fax consisted of a press release, welcoming the budget and, sensationally, a two-page document which outlined the main provisions of the budget – almost four hours before Finance Minister Ruairi Quinn would rise to address the Dáil!

THE IMPACT

It quickly emerged that a genuine error had occurred, but the opposition, particularly Fianna Fáil – still hurting after losing power so dramatically just a couple of months earlier – screamed blue murder. The previous year, Hogan had called for the resignation of Transport, Energy and Communications Minister Brian Cowen, when it was revealed that Cowen had a small shareholding in a mining company. Now it was payback time. 'He has to go if standards mean anything to the Labour Party and to Mr Bruton, who puts himself forward as a politician of probity,' Cowen said.

Despite the furore in the Dáil on budget night, Bruton dismissed suggestions that he would seek Hogan's resignation. Nobody seriously believed that he would have to go. There had only been three resignations from high office during the previous twenty years – two Taoisigh and one minister of state – and they were forced resignations. The norm in these situations was for the relevant minister to tough it out and the storm would finally blow over. However, the following day, Hogan shocked the Dáil by doing what it was assumed no Irish politician would ever countenance – resigning on a point of honour. He had been a Junior Minister for just seven weeks – one of the briefest tenures in the history of the State.

In his statement to the Dáil, Hogan apologised 'unreservedly' for what had happened. He stressed that it was a 'genuine mistake', stating: 'Without detracting from the seriousness of the situation, my colleagues must accept that nobody would attempt to leak a confidential document by faxing it to the press with their name attached'.

Hogan explained that his statement welcoming the budget was prepared in his office and completed at 11.45am. It was intended to release this one-page statement – which was on green-coloured paper – at the end of the Finance Minister's speech. At the same time, a second document – made up of two white pages – was prepared. This document contained 'summary elements of the budget statement and was due for release at the conclusion of the Minister's speech', he said. The document was to form the basis of a budget briefing Hogan had been scheduled to give to his parliamentary party later that evening. Hogan described how a document was presented to him in his office containing three pages. He was in a rush to be present for a debate in the Dáil chamber at the time and hurriedly looked at both the green page and the second and third pages, before approving them. 'I assumed that my special adviser was aware, as I was, that the three pages represented two documents and that they were intended for separate political purposes. However, in my desire to go quickly into the Chamber I regrettably did not leave full instructions that none of the material was to be released until after the budget speech of the Minister for Finance. This lack of clarity on my part caused confusion and both documents were issued as one in error to the news editors, starting with the two evening papers, at 12.15pm,' Hogan told the Dáil, stressing that the intention was to circulate only the green-coloured single page after Ruairí Quinn had finished speaking.

Half an hour after the material had been faxed, Hogan was informed by the government chief whip that budget material had been prematurely released and he immediately took action to prevent further circulation. To his credit, Hogan did not try and pass the blame to his adviser. 'Lack of clarity on my part in instructions to my political adviser resulted in this unfortunate incident. I assure the House I am fully aware of the seriousness of this matter and I take full responsibility for it,' he said, adding again that it was 'entirely a genuine error'. Hogan also admitted sending the budget proposals to the Fine Gael press office on the strict condition that the information would be kept secure until the budget speech was over. He said he understood this to be the 'practice of previous administrations'.

Hogan concluded that 'to avoid any possibility of damaging a Government led by the Taoiseach, Deputy John Bruton, a man of the utmost decency and understanding, I have tendered my resignation from Government and it has been accepted. The decision to resign is entirely my own'. The conclusion of his statement was greeted in the Dáil by spontaneous applause. Opposition leader Bertie Ahern paid tribute to Hogan 'for his honourable and courageous decision', adding that 'unfortunately, he has been made the fall guy for something which happened in recent days'. PD leader Mary Harney also described it as an 'honourable decision', adding: 'I am certain that Deputy Phil Hogan was not responsible for the extensive leaks in recent days'.

The irony of the whole affair was that given the level of leakage about the budget, Hogan's two-page document contained virtually nothing new. Yet Hogan paid the ultimate price for a genuine error. The following day's editorial in *The Irish Times* said it was 'difficult not to feel some sympathy' for Hogan, whom it described as 'a decent and honourable man who is a victim of his own political naivete'. However, it added that Bruton had no alternative but to accept Hogan's resignation. To do otherwise would renege on the government's commitment to openness, transparency and accountability in public life.

Although he lost ministerial office, the incident did not damage Hogan's career in the longer term. He became one of the party's most senior figures, who is likely to be offered a cabinet position if and when Fine Gael return to government.

Uno Duce, Una Voce

PJ Mara

THE BACKGROUND

It was early summer in 1984 and Charlie Haughey was where he least liked being – on the opposition benches. Although not in government, Haughey did have some reasons to be cheerful. After surviving three leadership challenges in the early part of the decade, his position as leader of Fianna Fáil was no longer under threat. Exhausted and drained from those tension-filled contests, few in the party had the appetite for any challenge to the leadership.

It was also in 1984 that Haughey had brought in his old friend PJ Mara as party press officer. Mara had been Haughey's companion in the early 1970s when Haughey had travelled the country attending Fianna Fáil functions, rebuilding his power base after the Arms Trial. Although Fiannna Fáil had first approached at least one heavy hitter from the media in relation to the position of press officer, the larger-than-life Mara proved an inspired choice for the job.

In his book *The Haughey File*, Stephen Collins wrote that

Mara took to the new job like a duck to water. Witty, irreverent and a superb raconteur, 'he kept the political journalists entertained with anecdotes and impersonations of the leading lights of the party, including his boss. His indiscretions soon became legendary but they were often so scabrous or libellous that they were unprintable. While they didn't do any harm to his boss, they conveyed the impression that Mara was telling all there was to know. As a result, journalists believed they were getting the inside track on what was happening in government but at the same time, they never got much usable information.'

Writing in *The Irish Times* in 1991, John Waters said that 'PJ doesn't so much do a job as weave a spell . . . His modus operandi is inseparable from his personality. He creates a web of bonhomie and laddishness around himself which is difficult to resist. He is an apparently bottomless source of witty remarks, epigrams and he is a brilliant mimic.' As well as being good company, Mara was also extremely intelligent and very well read. However, his relaxed style and his knowledge of history were about to land him in trouble.

The report of the New Ireland Forum – the body established a year earlier to attempt to create a unified position for all the constitutional nationalist parties in Ireland – was published in May 1984. It proposed three models for the North: a united Ireland, joint authority by the Irish and British governments or a federal solution. Although Haughey had accepted the inclusion of the latter two options, as soon as the report was published he dismissed them, arguing that only a united Ireland would bring peace to the North. The other parties – including the SDLP – were horrified at this virtual upstaging of the report. There was also some disquiet within Fianna Fáil that Haughey had taken this line without any debate within the party. Senator

Eoin Ryan demanded a meeting of the parliamentary party to discuss the issue. During that meeting, long-time Haughey foe Des O'Malley criticised the stifling of debate within the party. Haughey moved quickly against O'Malley, demanding that the party whip be withdrawn. This was passed after a vote of the parliamentary party by 56-16. The final elements of dissent in Fianna Fáil had been crushed. Haughey, for probably the first time since he became leader almost five years earlier, was in complete control of the party.

THE GAFFE

Mara, briefing political correspondents on the story, famously used the old Italian fascist slogan 'Uno Duce, Una Voce' (one leader, one voice) to sum up the new mood of the party. In case anybody didn't get the reference, he added: 'And, in other words, we are having no more nibbling at my leader's bum'.

THE IMPACT

In the following weekend's edition of the *Sunday Press*, the 'Uno Duce, Una Voce' quote was referred to in an analysis piece by political correspondent Geraldine Kennedy. It wasn't long before the phrase caught on and entered the political vernacular. Two days after the *Sunday Press* piece, Haughey's nemesis Conor Cruise O'Brien warmed to the theme in his column in *The Irish Times*. Opening with the words 'Uno Duce, Una Voce'

– Benito Mussolini, O'Brien wrote: 'One leader, one voice. That's the way it was with the fascists from 1923 to 1944 and that's the way it is with Fianna Fáil today'. He added that 'it's not me' that was calling Charles Haughey a fascist. 'The man who compared his own party leader's position on dissent to that of the late Duce was Mr PJ Mara – yes that PJ Mara, Mr Haughey's closest political confidant and currently – and by no coincidence – Fianna Fáil's acting press secretary'. Like a cat who had just got the cream, O'Brien continued: 'So you can't say you haven't been warned. The whole style of Fianna Fáil is now not so much specifically fascist as all purpose totalitarian dredged in leader worship and sycophancy.' He added that a recent motion introduced by Haughey and passed unanimously at the Fianna Fáil parliamentary party meeting – congratulating the party leader on his own contribution to the forum – was comparable to Breshnev's conferring of the Lenin Prize for literature 'on his own unreadable memoirs'.

Concluding on a more serious note, Cruise-O'Brien said: 'there is nothing funny about the current state of Fianna Fáil when Mussolini is being quoted with approval by the leader's spokesman'.

Government politicians were quick to seek to make political capital. Fine Gael candidate in Dublin for the European elections, Mary Banotti, reminded journalists that it was a quote from Mussolini. In the Dáil, the following day, Fine Gael Junior Minister George Birmingham, speaking on a guillotine motion, said he knew 'that Deputy [Bertie] Ahern is Whip to a party who adopt a novel and distinctive approach to internal party debate. I realise he is the Whip of a party who take the view that matters are best decided on the basis of one leader, one voice. In the event of anyone being unsure as to the meaning of *uno duce, una voce,* the party press officer, a constituent of mine and sometime Senator, PJ Mara, was available to interpret. He explained that the phrase so far as Fianna Fáil were concerned meant that no one was to nibble at his Leader's bum'. Irate letter writers to the newspapers claimed it was proof positive that Fianna Fáil demands absolute subservience to the party leader. The comment also came up at that week's meeting of the Fianna Fáil parliamentary party meeting.

Needless to say, Haughey was not impressed. In *The Haughey File,* Stephen Collins said Haughey reacted by screaming at Mara: 'You go into that room where they all hate me, and you give them this'. However, relations were quickly mended between the two, who were reportedly on the 'best of terms' again by the end of the week. Mara, for his part, pointed out that the media had missed his clever allusion to Fine Gael's Blueshirt era. Incorrigible as ever, he was soon referring to his boss as 'the Caudillo' – a name given to the South American political-military leaders who rose from the 19th-century wars of Independence – rather than Duce.

And while the 'Uno Duce, Una Voce' comment did backfire on Mara in the short term – giving the party's critics a stick to beat it with – most people realised the comment was tongue-in-cheek. It also helped turn Mara into a national figure. One of the few figures in politics known almost exclusively by his first name – or, in his case, initials – PJ went on to have a hugely successful career as government press secretary and then afterwards in the private sector.

Red, White and Blew It

Garret FitzGerald

THE BACKGROUND

In the 1980s, politics was dominated by the two most able politicians of their generation – Charlie Haughey and Garret FitzGerald. While Haughey was destined for high office from the late 1950s, FitzGerald was very much an atypical politician, despite coming from a prestigious political family. A brilliant intellect, 'Garret the Good', as he became known, would have been highly suited to a life in academia and was, in the words of Raymond Smith in his book Garret the Enigma – 'the very model of the confused woolly-headed professor'.

During one general election campaign, he was famously captured by a photographer wearing odd shoes. He had risen early and because he did not want to disturb his beloved wife Joan, he had not turned on the light before reaching for his shoes. Although highly personable and outgoing, like many brilliant intellects, he sometimes lacked the common touch, a touch which is the central component of Irish general election campaigns.

During the February 1982 general election campaign, FitzGerald visited Cork North West, probably the best organised Fine Gael constituency in the country at the time. Stephen O'Byrnes in his book *Hiding Behind a Face – Fine Gael under FitzGerald* wrote that the Fine Gael leader was welcomed to the constituency like an Irish chief. Bonfires blazed and FitzGerald was led into Macroom, Millstreet and Charleville by burning torches. 'It was an evening of passion, colour and drama,' O'Byrnes wrote.

THE GAFFE

Standing on the steps of the bus in Millstreet, FitzGerald thanked the people for the welcome and urged them to vote on election day. Somebody in the crowd then threw up a large red and white teddy bear. A huge cheer went up and the Fine Gael leader held up the teddy. However, he was clearly puzzled by something and asked the crowd: 'is there any significance in the colours?', to which came a groaning response: 'Dere de Cork colours boy'. 'Ah yes, yes indeed', FitzGerald responded.

THE IMPACT

It was a true howler. To arrive in, arguably, the foremost GAA county in the country and not recognise the blood and bandages was a big no-no. Imagine, for example, if Tony Blair visited

Manchester and failed to recognise the Manchester United jersey. As Stephen O'Byrnes put it: 'For all his faults, Charles Haughey would not have had to ask what was the significance of the red and white.' Raymond Smith noted that it was 'all like the lost world of the Incas' to FitzGerald.

And yet, if anything, such gaffes only added to his allure. FitzGerald did lose that February 1982 election but this electoral defeat was due to the unpopularity of Fine Gael's budget (see Chapter 18). By the end of the year, he was back as Taoiseach, sensationally bringing his party to within five seats of Fianna Fáil. He took Fine Gael from 43 seats in 1977 to 70 seats in the general election of November 1982 which, even allowing for the increase in the number of TDs in the Dáil, was an amazing turnabout in the party's fortunes.

Electorally, FitzGerald brought Fine Gael further than anybody has before or since. Part of Fine Gael's strength at the time was down to an anti-Haughey sentiment but there is no question that FitzGerald captured the imagination of voters. Smith summed it up well when he wrote: 'Garret is Garret warts and all. Everyone loves him all the more for the absent Professor-like qualities, as the son loves a father who may be helpless around the house, unable to change a fuse or cook a meal when mother is away. Garret's faults stem not from a too-human weakness that has brought good men down but rather a Clouseau-like fumbling and a falling-over-himself in the figurative sense that has made him distinctive among Irish politicians of the present day.'

While it is impossible, for example, to see the campaign of a US presidential candidate surviving the wearing of odd shoes, FitzGerald wasn't damaged by such stories because ultimately he was seen by voters as a great intellect and a man of great integrity. Smith reckoned that the public forgave and accepted those foibles because they saw him as a true academic, 'a man as it were in temporary exile, for the good of the nation, from his natural abode – a chair in some university'.

There was a nice postscript to the Millstreet gaffe. Nine months later, during the year's second general election campaign, FitzGerald visited Kerry, where Jimmy Deenihan – captain of the Kerry team that had won the county's fourth All Ireland in a row the year before – was standing for Fine Gael. To ensure there was no repeat of what happened with the Cork colours, the party's election planners repeatedly drummed into FitzGerald on the way down to the Kingdom that the Kerry colours were green and gold. When Garret came out for his walkabout, he was handed the number two jersey that Deenihan had worn against Offaly in the All Ireland final, and he was heard to remark knowingly, 'Ah, the Green and Gold'.

The Minister for Fornica . . .

Michael D Higgins

THE BACKGROUND

It was October 2005 and during the morning's Order of Business in the Dáil, Labour TD Michael D Higgins, in his role as the party's Foreign Affairs spokesman, was on his feet. A highly skilled debater, Higgins asked Tanaiste Mary Harney when exactly Ireland would ratify the UN Convention against Corruption and the International Convention on the Protection of the Rights of All Migrant Workers and Members of their Families. The Tanaiste reminded Higgins that he had raised the issue the previous week with the Minister for Foreign Affairs, Dermot Ahern, and that the Minister would have to communicate with the deputy. It was heavy duty and serious international business, but it was about to get a lot lighter.

THE GAFFE

Higgins responded: 'The Minister for Fornica . . . Foreign Affairs . . .' – inadvertently almost giving one of the most prestigious positions in the Irish government a new, more downmarket title.

THE IMPACT

Like an unruly classroom, the Dáil erupted with laughter. Higgins turned to his colleagues on the Labour benches, asking: 'What did I say?' Arts, Sports and Tourism Minister John O'Donoghue wondered aloud: 'I wonder who would get that job?' Undeterred by the cackling, Higgins continued his line of questioning, asking the Tanaiste if the government 'intended to ratify the United Nations Convention against Corruption?' However, he referred back to his slip of the tongue and prompted further hilarity when he said: 'I apologise for my misuse of language which was a consequence of Ireland's loss in yesterday's soccer match'. The previous night Ireland had failed to qualify for the 2006 World Cup Finals after drawing nil-all with Switzerland.

While football can do funny things to grown men, the explanation didn't do much to explain how fornication (qualification? nation? Four-four-two?) could be mixed up with foreign affairs. It did, however, provide some comic relief to help lift the air of depression after the Irish team's disappointment the previous night.

'Michael D mixing up his perfectly formed words is indeed an unprecedented event in the lifetime of a Dáil. For him to suddenly succumb to an attack of the Berties while speaking in the chamber is most unlike Labour's pet professor,' Miriam Lord wrote in the next day's *Irish Independent*.

Lord went on to recall a comical example of a deputy getting his colleague's name mixed up. The incident occurred when Progressive Democrat TD Mae Sexton was trying to enter a debate in the Dáil a couple of years previously and was duly called upon by Labour's Seamus Pattison, who was in the chair. The problem was that Pattison called on 'Mae West,' and when Sexton remained in her seat, it prompted, Lord wrote, 'Seamus to bellow with no small amount of feeling, 'Deputy Mae West!'

There was also the famous time in the Dáil when Albert Reynolds completely accidentally referred to John Bruton as John Unionist. Many of Bruton's opponents in Fianna Fáil thought the comment hit the nail perfectly on the head.

'But so was Hitler'

Ruairi Quinn

THE BACKGROUND

It was November 1995 and the country was about to vote on a referendum changing the constitution to remove the ban on divorce. Although an earlier referendum on divorce in 1986 had been soundly defeated, Ireland had changed dramatically in the intervening nine years and the power of a scandal-hit church had declined considerably. Opinion polls in the months leading up to the referendum campaign consistently pointed to a comfortable victory for the 'Yes' vote. However, as the day of the vote, 24 November, approached, it was clear the confidence that there would be a resounding victory for the pro-divorce campaign was woefully misplaced. The rainbow government of Fine Gael, Labour and Democratic Left was running a lacklustre campaign.

In contrast, the anti-divorce side was anything but lacklustre – they were raising fears that the introduction of divorce would end the constitutional protection for the first family in favour of the second partner. There were two anti-divorce groups, but it was William Binchy and the Anti-Divorce Campaign that was doing the most damage to the 'Yes' campaign. Binchy, Regius Professor of Law at Trinity College Dublin and an intellectual heavyweight, was yet again proving to be an excellent tactician and communicator, with the ability to explain complex issues very simply and in a calm, courteous manner.

Charlie Haughey used to say privately that Binchy, brother of author Maeve Binchy, had defeated the 1986 divorce referendum almost single-handedly. And nine years on, he was clearly the star performer on either side of the campaign. In a number of debates, he very obviously got the better of increasingly nervy government ministers, who seemed powerless to stop the once massive lead of the 'Yes' campaign being continuously whittled away. To make matters worse for the government, an appeal to the Supreme Court by Green MEP Patricia McKenna to stop the government spending taxpayers' money to advocate a particular result in the referendum had succeeded.

THE GAFFE

Just over a week before polling day, the Fine Gael, Labour and Democratic Left representatives of Dublin South East held a press conference. As Labour TD for the constituency, Finance Minister Ruairi Quinn was present. During the conference, Quinn referred to Professor Binchy, stating that he was a very clever man 'but so was Hitler'.

THE IMPACT

It was a near disastrous intervention by Quinn, handing a massive PR coup to the anti-divorce side at a crucial time. For starters, the remarks had the effect of burying hardline comments – which should have been highly damaging to the 'No' campaign – from a bishop that the sacraments would be withheld from people in second relationships. John O'Reilly of the Anti-Divorce Campaign said Quinn's remarks were the logical culmination of the government's campaign, adding: 'Personal abuse is no substitute for addressing our arguments'.

The government was on the defensive. Quinn's cabinet colleagues quickly moved to distance themselves from the remarks. Minister for Equality and Law Reform Mervyn Taylor commiserated with Binchy, stating that as someone who had personal remarks made about him during the campaign, he wished Quinn's comments had not been made. Another senior Minister, Michael Noonan, and Minister for State Liz McManus also disassociated themselves from the outburst.

To be fair to Quinn, he immediately issued a fulsome apology to Binchy. 'I made an intemperate remark about Professor William Binchy at a press conference this afternoon. I deeply regretted this remark, which was totally unwarranted, as soon as I made it and I apologise unreservedly to Mr Binchy. I hope that Professor Binchy will take no hurt or offence from my tasteless remark.'

The editorial in *The Irish Times* the next day wrote that Quinn had 'probably done more to earn support for William Binchy's position than anything else in likening his cleverness to that of Adolf Hitler'.

An analysis piece in the same newspaper said the sharpness of the comments was 'seen to reflect government anger and frustration over a continuing slippage in the opinion polls', adding that 'rather than help the cause, however, it plunged ministers into a frenzy of hand wringing'.

It concluded: 'The episode stopped the coalition campaign dead in the water. From a position where Mr Quinn had led the government assault on the financial figures of the 'No' campaign last week, describing them as 'unfounded' and 'lies', the coalition parties were becalmed, apologising for offending their most dangerous opponent.'

However, while unquestionably a major gaffe, the remarks ultimately did not prove fatal to the 'Yes' campaign. The controversy surrounding them died fairly quickly, prompting one commentator, writing some years later, to speculate if the furore would have blown over so quickly if a bishop had made the same remark about somebody on the 'Yes' campaign. We will never know the answer to that.

What we do know is that the government finally bucked up its campaign over the last few days and it proved just about enough. The country voted by an incredibly tight margin – 0.56% or just over 9,000 votes – to pass the referendum removing the ban on divorce that had been enshrined in the constitution. Given that all the main political parties had supported a 'Yes' vote, it was a remarkably close result. Indeed, but for exceptionally bad weather on polling day in the west of Ireland where the 'No' campaign was strongest, the result might have been different.

Burning Bridges

Mary McAleese

THE BACKGROUND

A Catholic from Northern Ireland, Mary McAleese, the Fianna Fáil candidate, was elected president in 1997, winning a resounding victory after one of the most bitterly contested presidential elections in the history of the State. Although her campaign promised to 'build bridges', McAleese's background was the subject of much attention in the run-up to the election with critics describing her as 'an unreconstructed Northern nationalist' who, in the words of Eoghan Harris, was 'basically a tribal time-bomb'.

However, in the Áras, McAleese proved to be anything but incendiary when it came to Northern Ireland. In fact, one of the most notable features of her first term as president were the close contacts she developed with loyalist leaders. Such was McAleese's popularity among voters that she was deemed to be unbeatable by the end of that term and she was returned unopposed for a second seven year stint as president.

THE GAFFE

In a radio interview in January 2005, on the 60th anniversary of the liberation of the Nazi concentration camp Auschwitz, McAleese spoke of the intolerance that led to ethnic hatred. She compared the Nazis' hatred of Jews with how Catholics were viewed in Northern Ireland.

'They [the Nazis] gave to their children an irrational hatred of Jews in the same way that people in Northern Ireland transmitted to their children an irrational hatred, for example, of Catholics, in the same way that people give to their children an outrageous and irrational hatred of those who are of different colour and all of those things.'

THE IMPACT

Predictably, unionist leaders were furious at the comments, regarding it as a case of bridge burning, rather than building. For McAleese's critics in the south, seven and a half years on from that divisive election campaign, there was a huge element of 'told you so'.

The DUP's Ian Paisley Jnr, not untypically, was one of the first into the fray. 'So much for bridge-building Mary. Her comments are completely irrational and are designed to insult the integrity of the Protestant community and damn an entire generation of Protestant people.'

The Ulster Unionists also criticised the remarks. Michael McGimpsey, a former minister in the North's executive, said it

was 'outrageous for Mary McAleese to equate the Holocaust with Northern Ireland. It shows firstly a total lack of understanding and sympathy for Jews under the Nazis, and secondly, a deep-seated sectarianism.'

Even among those sympathetic to McAleese and what she was trying to say, there was a view that the comparison was ill-judged. Former Labour leader Ruairi Quinn said he fully accepted the general point the president was making but added: 'However, in the Irish context, it is important for all public figures at all levels to acknowledge that no section of the community in Northern Ireland has been the sole victim of sectarianism'.

Northern nationalist leaders defended the president. The SDLP leader Mark Durkan argued that she was in no way trying to equate any of the prejudices in Northern Ireland with the systematic genocide of the Nazi regime. Durkan also criticised unionists for condemning the president when they were slow to confront sectarian attacks and abuse aimed at the children attending the Holy Cross school in Belfast or Catholics going to Mass in Harryville in Ballymena.

Sinn Féin's Alex Maskey claimed the unionist reaction to the president's comments was 'hysterical'.

McAleese's spokeswoman attempted to calm the situation, insisting the statement was not intended to insult Protestants and was made in the context of a discussion on the Holocaust. 'The President was speaking about how the effects of hatred and intolerance are seen around the world and how they can impact on our children and one of the examples she used was Northern Ireland,' she said. 'Her comments were never intended to single out the Protestant people of Northern Ireland.'

McAleese herself apologised on RTÉ that day, saying she was deeply sorry for the remarks. 'The words I used were clumsy,' she said. 'The last thing I would want to do is to create the impression that sectarianism came from only one side of the community.'

The apology did take some of the heat out of the controversy. Ulster Unionist leader David Trimble welcomed her comments. 'I'm glad that there has been an apology, because I considered the remarks remarkably ill-judged. It is most unlike her to make a mistake of that nature, a mistake because it trivialises the experience of European Jewry and trivialises the Holocaust and also causes considerable offence in Northern Ireland.

'While no doubt that is true of some people, it is not right to lump together the Protestants of Northern Ireland and accuse them of this and to ignore the fact that a considerable amount of hatred exists within some members of the Catholic community,' he said.

The Orange Order welcomed the apology but said it was too early to reconsider their decision, made after the initial remarks, to cancel a meeting with the president. 'We are glad that she has responded so quickly. At our headquarters we have had more calls on this than most other things over the last few years. Her comments have pushed a lot of buttons in the north,' a spokeswoman said, adding: 'Mary McAleese has done a lot to build bridges but just one thing can do a lot to destroy that. We welcome that she came out and apologised so quickly.'

However, the full impact of the furore did not completely die down. The president had to postpone a visit, scheduled for the following month, to the loyalist heartland of the Shankill Road in Belfast. While the senior South Belfast loyalist Jackie McDonnell said: 'No matter what she said or whatever way it was taken, it wasn't meant that way', Progressive Unionist leader David Ervine said the damage was long term.

It was clear that resentment remained in some quarters in the North. Over a year later, McAleese was the subject of a strongly-worded attack by DUP leader Ian Paisley. He accused the president of having a deep hatred of Northern Ireland and said she should be subject to the same protocols as any other foreign head of state. 'The fact that she takes protection from the PSNI but refuses to go into a police station when they are changing shows how deep her hatred is of Northern Ireland,' Paisley said.

However, there was an interesting postscript to the controversy in March 2006 when British Prime Minister Tony Blair compared Protestant bigotry with Islamic extremism. Defending British involvement in Iraq and Afghanistan, Blair said: 'There are those – perfectly decent-minded people – who say the extremists who commit these [Islamic] acts of terrorism are not true Muslims. And of course, they are right. They are no more proper Muslims than the Protestant bigot who murders a Catholic in Northern Ireland is a proper Christian. But unfortunately he is still a Protestant bigot. To say his religion is irrelevant is both completely to misunderstand his motive and to refuse to face up to the strain of extremism within his religion that has given rise to it.'

Blair's comments triggered a similar reaction to McAleese's remarks in some quarters. Ian Paisley Jnr accused Blair of 'character assassination'. However, some more moderate unionist commentators conceded that, coming from a non-Catholic and the prime minister of the United Kingdom of Great Britain and Northern Ireland, the remarks could not be easily dismissed as 'deep-seated sectarianism'.

A Dick-In-The-Box

Charlie Haughey

THE BACKGROUND

Early 1982. The Fine Gael and Labour coalition had collapsed over the infamous 'VAT on children's shoes' budget (see Chapter 18). In the ensuing general election, Charlie Haughey's Fianna Fáil failed to win an overall majority, taking 81 seats – just short of the required 83 mark, even with the vote of Independent Fianna Fáil deputy Neil Blaney. With the help of the votes of Independent TD Tony Gregory – courtesy of the Gregory Deal – and three Workers' Party deputies, Haughey was elected Taoiseach for the second time.

However, Haughey knew this victory could be short-lived and his government was extremely vulnerable to a defeat in the Dáil, which could end his grip on power. Haughey and his close associates looked at the options for improving the Dáil arithmetic. They considered offering the Ceann Comhairle position to a Fine Gael or Labour TD – thereby removing one opposition vote from the equation. But there was another more radical option. Michael O'Kennedy had resigned his post in

Brussels, so the government had to fill the plum IR£70,000 a year job of EEC Commissioner. Haughey could give the job to a Fine Gael TD, who would have to resign his/her seat and with a bit of luck, Fianna Fáil would win the next by-election, giving it a de-facto majority if Blaney's vote was included.

THE GAFFE

In their acclaimed book on Haughey, entitled *The Boss*, Joe Joyce and Peter Murtagh wrote that the idea of awarding the Commissionership to an opposition TD was 'so politically outrageous, so daring – almost swashbuckling – that even Fine Gael people spoke of it as a joke in the immediate aftermath of the election. They thought it so preposterous that not even Haughey would try it. But as the election results became clear, this was exactly what Haughey was considering.' An informal approach was reportedly made to Sligo-Leitrim TD Ted Nealon, who made it clear he was not interested.

Haughey's attention then quickly focused on Dick Burke, Fine Gael TD for Dublin West, a former Minister and also – crucially – a former Commissioner. The view was that Burke was not particularly happy with being asked to run in Dublin West, where he was regarded as a fish out of water. Burke was sounded out unofficially and after a number of meetings, he was formally offered the job. According to The Boss, when Haughey told his cabinet about his decision, Minister for Labour Gene FitzGerald looked at him and said: 'A master stroke, Taoiseach, 'tis only yourself could think of it'.

However, not everyone sitting around the cabinet table was convinced. Fine Gael held the edge over Fianna Fáil in Dublin

West, where they had three seats, and it would be very difficult for the government to win the by-election. The whole deal looked to be off when Burke got savaged at a Fine Gael parliamentary party meeting. After a stroll around the grounds of Leinster House garden with Garret FitzGerald, he agreed to withdraw his acceptance of the offer, later issuing a statement to that effect. However, the following day, Burke changed his mind again and, following a trip to Brussels, agreed to take the position. Fine Gael immediately accused Haughey of simple political opportunism. Within Fianna Fáil, there was irritation in some quarters at seeing such a prestigious position being given to a Fine Gael man. Among Haughey's opponents in the party there were concerns that the move would be perceived as 'stroke pulling', further damaging Fianna Fáil's image.

Those concerns were well placed, as were the worries of those in the party who believed Dublin West would be a tough constituency for Fianna Fáil to win. Fianna Fáil seemed to have the stronger candidate in Eileen Lemass, a 49-year old widow, who – like Haughey – had married one of Sean Lemass' children. Lemass, who had lost her seat in the general election the previous February, was more experienced than Fine Gael's candidate Liam Skelly, a political novice.

Fianna Fáil also took advantage of being in government to deliver a whole range of goodies to the constituency, including a new factory for Blanchardstown, new schools and community centres, promises of a new road bypassing the bottlenecks of Lucan, Leixlip, Maynooth and Kilcock, and – most infamously on the eve of the poll – a truckload of new trees for a housing estate in Clonsilla where residents had complained about the state in which developers had left the area. (The day after the by-election, the trees in the housing estate were dug up by the people from whom they had been borrowed and taken away.) With her experience and the government's largesse, Lemass was odds-on favourite, but it wasn't to be for Fianna Fáil. Although Lemass finished just ahead of Skelly on the first count, it wasn't enough. The Fine Gael man was always going to do better on transfers and he comfortably won the seat by over 2,000 votes.

THE IMPACT

As Joyce and Murtagh put it in *The Boss*, the masterstroke had come unstuck. Haughey had given away probably the most plum job in his possession and he got nothing in return for it. His government was as vulnerable as ever. Worse still, the perception of the whole affair among the wider public was more 'stroke' than 'masterstroke', adding to the negative perception of Haughey among many voters.

The impact on the public finances was also negative. Before the by-election the government had introduced a new more generous tax allowance for those paying higher PRSI rates. It also headed off a threatened rise in mortgage rates by offering building societies cheap loans and lower taxes. Increases in children's allowances, due in July, were brought forward to May. 'The by-election had cost the exchequer, directly or indirectly, an enormous amount of money. The PRSI concession could not be said to have been caused solely by the by-election, but the atmosphere created by the impending poll helped to bring it about. That cost the state IR£45m in lost revenue. Commitments to subsidise mortgage rates until the following September and to speed up payments of children's allowances also disrupted the budget targets,' wrote Joyce and Murtagh.

If the gamble had paid off and Lemass had taken the seat, Haughey's decision to offer the Commissionership to Burke might have been regarded as one of the most audacious coups in Irish political history. But it didn't and given the evidence of Fine Gael's strength in the constituency that was available before offering the Commissionership to Burke, it must be regarded as a monumental gaffe.

Within a few months, the Dáil arithmetic caught up with Haughey and Fianna Fáil. Down two votes in the Dáil, due to the death of Bill Loughnane and the illness of Jim Gibbons, and without the votes of the Workers' Party – who reacted against the government's tough new economic strategy – the government lost a no-confidence motion, causing a general election. The result was a disaster for Fianna Fáil. Fine Gael came within five seats of Fianna Fáil and along with Labour was in a position to form a government with a comfortable majority. Haughey would spend the next four years in opposition.

High Jinks on the Train

John Jinks

THE BACKGROUND

It was the summer of 1927 and for the first time since the formation of the new State, Cumann na nGaedheal's hold on power appeared to be slipping. The newly created Fianna Fáil party contested the June general election and secured 44 seats, just three short of Cumann na nGaedheal's total. However, Fianna Fáil was still outside the Dáil, refusing to take the hated Oath of Allegiance. De Valera planned to force a referendum on the Oath – which would certainly have led to its abolition – by invoking a clause in the constitution obliging the government to hold a referendum on any issue that produced a petition from 75,000 voters.

However, the Irish political scene was turned upside down by the assassination in July of the strong man of the government, Kevin O'Higgins. The President of the Executive Council (as the office of the Taoiseach was then known), William T. Cosgrave, reacted by introducing an act obliging all Dáil candidates to pledge to take the Oath and bringing forward measures to change the constitution within eight years, in order to remove the article that would have allowed Fianna Fáil to force a referendum on the Oath.

Although he seemed to be backed into a corner, de Valera came up with his 'empty formula' solution. He devised a ceremony whereby Fianna Fáil TDs signed the book containing the Oath, but covered the words while signing, placed the Bible face down in the furthest corner of the room and insisted they were not taking any oath. Fianna Fáil was now in the Dáil and suddenly the pressure was firmly on Cosgrave and his government, which was now in a minority with just 47 of the 153 seats. De Valera did not want to go into government straightaway, but he was not adverse to toppling his bitter political rivals in Cumann na nGaedheal. He offered support to the Labour Party, who had 22 deputies, if its leader, Tom Johnson, could put a coalition together. Johnson duly opened negotiations with some of the smaller groupings, including the National League – a party founded the year before by William Redmond and Thomas O'Donnell, which supported close relations with the UK and continued membership of the British Commonwealth. Backed by many unionists and former supporters of the once dominant Irish Parliamentary Party, it had already won eight seats in the general election. The parties got as far as agreeing on a cabinet at a meeting in a hotel in Enniskerry, Co Wicklow with Johnson as President of the Executive Council.

A motion of no-confidence was scheduled for 16 August 1927. Given the presence of Fianna Fáil's 44 deputies, his motion seemed guaranteed to succeed. Newspapers predicted that the government would be defeated by 73 votes to 69. Such was the level of confidence among the opposition that one

Labour TD, TJ O'Connell, was not even asked to come home from a teachers' conference in Canada for the vote.

THE GAFFE

On the date of the vote, government TD – and former unionist MP – Major Bryan Cooper bumped into the National League TD for Sligo, John Jinks. The two men had something in common. Cooper had fought in Gallipoli, while Jinks was an ex-serviceman, who had helped recruit men for the British Army during the First World War. Cooper quickly detected Jinks' unhappiness at the prospect of voting with de Valera and invited him to lunch to discuss the matter further. What happened next has never been firmly established, but the rumour was that Cooper plied Jinks with drink over the lunch and then escorted him in a befuddled state to Westland Row train station. While the vote was taken on the no-confidence motion later that afternoon in the Dáil, Jinks was snoozing on the train as it trundled through the midlands. With Jinks absent, the vote was tied at 71 votes for and against the motion. The Ceann Comhairle, Michael Hayes, gave his casting vote in favour of the government. Cosgrave and his cabinet were saved.

THE IMPACT

The incident was one of the greatest sensations in the early political life of the new State. There was wild speculation about the reasons for Jinks' absence (was he spirited away or was he kidnapped?) and it made newspaper headlines across Europe and the US, including *Time Magazine*. While he has gone down as one of the most hapless TDs in the history of the State, others have argued that his absence from such a key vote was a deliberate expression of his political views.

Responding to the controversy created, Jinks told reporters he had gone to Dublin with instructions from two thirds of his supporters to vote for the government. 'I was neither kidnapped nor spirited away. I simply walked out of the Dáil when I formed my own opinion after listening to a good many speeches. I cannot understand the sensation nor can I understand the meaning or object of the many reports circulated. What I did was done after careful consideration of the entire situation. I have nothing to regret for my action. I am glad I was the single individual who saved the situation for the Government, and perhaps, incidentally, for the country. I believe I acted for its good,' he said.

Whatever his intentions, there is no doubt that Jinks changed political history. Labour was never again to come as close to being the main government party. Who knows what impact it could have had on the party's fortunes if it had not been 'Jinked' in August 1927 and Tom Johnson had become President of the Executive Council. As it was, the party's window of opportunity quickly closed. The following month Cosgrave dissolved the Dáil and in the general election Labour lost nine seats, while Cumann na nGaedheal gained 15. Fianna Fáil gained 13 seats. Although a Fianna Fáil government was now only a matter of time, Cumann na nGaedheal, along with its allies, had a secure majority to govern for another five years. The National League, meanwhile, had a disastrous election, returning with just two

TDs. The party went bankrupt the following year and was disbanded in 1931 – quite a change of fortune given that it was destined for government before Jinks went 'awol'.

Jinks himself stood as an independent candidate in that election, but his vote dropped by a third and he lost his seat. Although his action ensured his place in history, he never made it back to Dáil Éireann. Perhaps not surprisingly, he later joined Cumann na nGaedheal and in 1928 he was elected to Sligo County Council. He was re-elected to the Council in 1934, but died in September of that year.

GUBU
Patrick Connolly AG

THE BACKGROUND

In July 1982, the country was in a state of shock following two killings in three days. First, Nurse Bridie Gargan was bludgeoned to death while sunbathing in the Phoenix Park and then three days later Westmeath farmer Donal Dunne was shot dead with his own gun. Within a week, the Gardaí had begun to link the two murders.

Ten days after Donal Dunne was shot, the country's Attorney General (AG), Patrick Connolly, had a visitor to his flat in Dalkey, on the southside of Dublin. The visitor, Malcolm MacArthur, had become friends with Connolly some years earlier after meeting through a mutual friend, Brenda Little. MacArthur and Little had a son together in the mid 1970s. According to Joe Joyce and Peter Murtagh's brilliant book *The Boss*, detailing Charlie Haughey's disastrous period in government in 1982, MacArthur told Connolly he expected to be in Ireland for a few days, sorting out a financial matter. Connolly assumed it was something to do with his grandmother's estate and offered him a bed in his flat if he wished to stay – an offer which MacArthur accepted.

THE GAFFE

Unknown to Connolly – and it is important to stress that the AG at no time had any knowledge of a problem surrounding his guest – MacArthur was the man Gardaí were hunting for in their investigation into the murders of Bridie Gargan and Donal Dunne. Four days after he moved in – in a twist that would seem far-fetched in a work of fiction – Connolly, his brother, nephew and MacArthur were chauffeured across Dublin in Connolly's Garda-driven state car to attend an All Ireland hurling semi-final in Croke Park. Connolly and his brother had seats in the VIP section, where the Garda Commissioner, Patrick McLaughlin, was also watching the game. MacArthur, the country's most wanted man, had a seat in the stand. But the net was closing in on him.

The following Friday – Friday the 13th, unlucky for some – Connolly left his office in government buildings and headed home. He was due to fly out on holidays the following day but his plans were to change dramatically. When he arrived at his flat in Dalkey, he was met by three detectives who asked him if there was a man staying there. According to *The Boss*, Connolly told them that his friend Malcolm MacArthur was staying there and in turn the detectives told him that MacArthur was wanted in connection with an armed robbery in Killiney (MacArthur had attempted to get money at gunpoint from a former US diplomat at his home in Killiney over a week earlier). Attempts by the detectives to buzz MacArthur on the intercom, telephone him and to open the door using keys proved unsuccessful.

MacArthur, however, finally opened the door to the flat at Connolly's request and the detectives entered to find MacArthur unarmed. *The Boss* recounts that Connolly walked in, looked at MacArthur and said: 'I don't know what this is about, Malcolm, but whatever it is, you are on your own'. Quizzed by the detectives, MacArthur led them to a storage compartment just under the roof and showed them a refuse bag, inside which was a shotgun. Connolly was amazed. He had no idea the gun was in his flat. It was only later that evening a shocked Connolly was told of murder charges facing MacArthur.

It was clear to the Gardaí that the AG was utterly innocent. At around 10pm that night, Connolly rang the Taoiseach Charlie Haughey at his island retreat of Inishvickillane, one of the Blasket Islands off the coast of west Kerry. 'He told Haughey what had happened but Haughey didn't seem to grasp the significance of events or didn't hear properly on the bad line. Connolly told him he was going on his holidays the following morning and Haughey didn't tell him not to. Haughey thought he was just being informed about the arrest, perhaps because he should congratulate the gardaí,' Joyce and Murtagh wrote in *The Boss*.

The following morning, the detectives called to Connolly's flat but 'Connolly was in no mood to talk to them'. Despite being pressed for a statement, Connolly argued he was an innocent party in the affair and could make a statement on his return. The detectives were forced to accept this and, incredibly, Connolly caught his flight to London, from where he would fly to New York. It was to prove a disastrous error of judgment. Later that day, MacArthur was charged with two murders and aggravated burglary at a special sitting of Dún Laoghaire district court. The address he gave to the court was the same as Connolly's.

THE IMPACT

Grotesque, Unbelievable, Bizzare and definitely Unprecedented. A man wanted for two murders found at the home of the AG, who had left the country the following day at the height of what is traditionally the quietest news month of all – the media had a field day. Haughey, on getting a briefing from his officials, realised the magnitude of what had unfolded and ordered that Connolly be contacted in London. When the two men spoke, Haughey asked him to return to Dublin but Connolly said he didn't want to, as he was on his holidays and about to depart for the US. Haughey agreed that Connolly could ring him again on landing in New York, with Haughey reportedly under the impression that the AG was about to board his flight.

However, Connolly stayed overnight in London and only flew to New York the following day. The headline in that day's final edition of the *Sunday Tribune* read: 'A-G flies out as murder suspect charged'. The you-know-what had hit the fan. Connolly touched down at JFK Airport to be greeted by Ireland's deputy consul general in New York and a media scrum. After speaking with Haughey by telephone, the AG accepted he would have to fly back to Dublin, which he did on Concorde to London –

where he was again besieged by reporters with BBC filming his arrival live on its main evening news – and then onto Dublin on an Irish Air Corps plane.

Connolly met with Haughey at the Taoiseach's Kinsealy home. The two men were agreed that resignation was the only option under the circumstances. A statement was drafted stressing Connolly's innocence but adding that because of his unique position under the constitution and the embarrassment caused to the government, it was his public duty to tender his resignation. This statement was released to the media in the early hours of Tuesday morning. Connolly went home to his flat in Dalkey. The following day he made his statement to Gardaí.

The damage caused to Haughey's government was enormous (see Chapter 38). Despite all the wild rumours that spread at the time, there was no cover up, but such was the magnitude of the story that the public's confidence and trust in the government evaporated. The four adjectives Haughey used to describe the affair – Grotesque, Unbelievable, Bizzare and Unprecedented – led to the invention of a new word GUBU, which was coined by Conor Cruise O'Brien, a long-time adversary of the Taoiseach.

Haughey's government of 1982 would forever be known as the 'GUBU government'. Today there is even a pub in Dublin called GUBU, although whether the mainly young clientele have any knowledge of the name's origin is a moot point.

The following January, MacArthur was sentenced to penal servitude for life when he pleaded guilty to Bridie Gargan's murder in a hearing in the Central Criminal Court which lasted about five minutes. However, by then Haughey's scandal-ridden government had lost power.

The Right Man
Charlie Haughey

THE BACKGROUND

It was August 1982 and one of the most explosive stories in Irish political history had just broken. The country had been shocked by two killings in three days. Nurse Bridie Gargan was bludgeoned to death while sunbathing in the Phoenix Park and three days later Westmeath farmer Donal Dunne was shot with his own gun. Then, sensationally, Malcolm MacArthur, the man wanted by Gardaí in connection with the murder investigation, was arrested at the Dalkey home of the Attorney General (AG) Patrick Connolly (see Chapter 37). The AG was completely unaware that Gardaí were searching for MacArthur – whom he had known socially for a number of years – when he had invited him to stay at his flat.

Despite the sensational development, Connolly actually departed on his pre-planned holiday the day after MacArthur's arrest. Connolly travelled to London and then on to New York the following day. But he quickly returned from New York as the storm of controversy intensified and he tendered his resignation from the position of Attorney General. MacArthur was charged with the two murders and with aggravated burglary.

The controversy was a major embarrassment for Charlie Haughey's government. An embattled Haughey famously described the series of events as 'grotesque, unbelievable, bizzare and unprecedented' – prompting Conor Cruise O'Brien to coin the acronym GUBU, a tag which that government was never able to shake off.

On the day that the AG resigned, Haughey hosted a press conference on public sector pay negotiations, but inevitably the media's focus was on Patrick Connolly and Malcolm MacArthur. Under intense pressure over his inept handling of the affair, Haughey was ill-at-ease with the questioning and was caught off guard on a number of occasions. Haughey admitted he had spoken to Connolly on the Friday night of MacArthur's arrest and that when he spoke to him the following day in London, he [Haughey] knew all the facts of the case and yet still agreed to Connolly flying to New York. This conflicted with what a Government Information Service spokesman had said earlier – that Haughey's first contact with Connolly had been on the Sunday when the Taoiseach spoke to him by telephone in New York. But worse was to come.

THE GAFFE

At one point during the press conference, Haughey was asked why nobody in the government had congratulated the Gardaí on their work. He replied: 'It was a very good piece of policework, slowly, painstakingly, putting the whole thing together and eventually finding the right man'. The comment was disastrous because MacArthur was legally entitled to the presumption of innocence until he was proved guilty of the charges brought against him. Haughey's comments risked prejudicing the outcome of the MacArthur trial and appeared to be clearly in contempt of court.

THE IMPACT

Haughey's advisors twigged there was a problem with the comment virtually straight away. Government press secretary Frank Dunlop discussed the remark with Haughey and informed news editors that the remark had been made inadvertently and that Haughey was horrified at the form of words he had mistakenly used. The offending words were not broadcast on the main RTÉ news bulletin, nor were they included on RTÉ Radio One's 6.30pm news magazine programme, which ran lengthy excerpts from the press conference.

Irish media organisations risked also being held in contempt of court if they broadcast the comments. However, the same restraints did not hold for foreign media. Both the BBC – on its television and radio bulletins – and ITN carried the crucial sentence from Haughey in their reports. Even in 1982, BBC and ITN news was available all along the east coast – where a jury for the murder trial would be sourced – while the entire country could access BBC radio.

The following day's newspapers cited legal sources saying a

comment made by the Taoiseach could constitute contempt of court. 'Such a comment is in my opinion damaging as the case is *sub judice*,' one lawyer was quoted as saying. 'I am very unhappy about the broadcasting of this comment on radio and TV,' said another. And, in *The Irish Times* the next day, it was reported that the Taoiseach faced legal action over the remark. It quoted MacArthur's solicitor as saying: 'Some action is being taken. Something is moving. It was a remark in contempt.' It speculated that an application could be made to the High Court with a request that the court should examine if there was a prima facie case that contempt had been committed. According to legal opinion, if the request was granted by the High Court, the Taoiseach could be brought before the court. If he was found guilty of contempt, he could be fined or imprisoned or both. It represented an appalling scenario for an already embattled Haughey.

However, fortunately for the Taoiseach, the attempt to have him cited for contempt was rejected by the High Court. Justice Costello said that contempt of court was a criminal offence, but the evidence indicated the remark made by Haughey was a 'slip of the tongue', although it had caused much concern. Costello also noted that journalists had been asked not to publish the remarks.

As Joe Joyce and Peter Murtagh later wrote in *The Boss*, the High Court's finding 'did not stop some people thinking that the [Haughey] remark was part of a huge conspiracy to keep the case out of the courts and thus protecting certain unnamed people, politicians and lawyers'. Of course, as Joyce and Murtagh pointed out, there was nothing whatsoever in these conspiracy theories, but it says a lot for the atmosphere surrounding that GUBU period that they gained some credence.

In January 1983, MacArthur was sentenced to penal servitude for life when he pleaded guilty to Bridie Gargan's murder at a hearing in the Central Criminal Court. Haughey got away with his major gaffe at the press conference – the implications of being cited for contempt would have been horrendous for him – but the whole MacArthur affair seriously damaged public confidence and trust in Haughey's government. Just a few months later the GUBU government fell after losing a crucial Dáil vote.

Sympathy for the Devil

Eamon de Valera

THE BACKGROUND

In 1945, after almost six years of bloody and terrible conflict, the Second World War was drawing to a close. Ireland, under the leadership of Eamon de Valera, had remained neutral throughout the war. The Taoiseach, with good reason, believed that any other policy would have split the country with disastrous consequences. Instead of suffering the horrors of war, Ireland had to endure 'The Emergency'.

However, despite Churchill's utterly groundless swipe after the conclusion of the war – about leaving the 'de Valera government to frolic with the German, and later the Japanese, representatives to their hearts' content', the reality was that the country was benevolently neutral in the Allies' favour. This included quietly passing on intelligence data to MI5. On 2 May, the suicide of Adolf Hitler in his Berlin bunker was announced in the Irish newspapers.

THE GAFFE

Later that day, de Valera, who was Minister for External Affairs (now Foreign Affairs) as well as Taoiseach, accompanied by the secretary of the Department of External Affairs, Joseph Walshe, called to the residence of the German ambassador, Edouard Hempel, at De Vesci Terrace, Monkstown on Dublin's southside to formally express condolences at Hitler's death. It is understood that Hempel warned him of the trouble his visit would cause to which de Valera responded: 'I do what I think is right'.

THE IMPACT

Right or not, the Allies reacted with horror and outrage at the decision to pay a formal call of condolence. De Valera's biographer, the Earl of Longford, later wrote that 'nothing that he did at any time in the war was so unpopular in allied countries'. De Valera's actions are still debated to this day, with critics noting that by early May 1945 the appalling atrocities that took place in German concentration camps were being shown around the world on newsreels.

An unrepentant de Valera did not give any explanation in public for his decision to call, because he felt this would have been interpreted as an admission that he had done something wrong, which he did not believe. Privately, though, in a letter to the Irish ambassador in Washington DC, Bob Brennan, de Valera said to have failed to call on Hempel 'would have been an act of unpardonable discourtesy to the German nation and to Dr Hempel himself'. He added: 'During the whole of the War, Dr Hempel's conduct was irreproachable. He was always friendly and invariably correct.' This, de Valera said, was 'in marked contrast' with the US ambassador to Ireland, David Gray, whom de Valera detested for his campaign to persuade Ireland to abandon neutrality and give bases to the Allies. 'I certainly was not going to add to his [Hempel's] humiliation in the hour of defeat,' de Valera said.

In the letter to Brennan, de Valera wrote that he expected his visit to Hempel to be 'played up to the utmost', adding: 'I could have had a diplomatic illness but, as you know, I would scorn that sort of thing'. He also wrote that not expressing condolences would have established a 'bad precedent', stating, 'It is important that it should never be inferred that these formal acts imply the passing of any judgments, good or bad'.

The argument still rages over whether diplomatic protocol could be given as a reason for expressing condolences on the death of Hitler. Shortly afterwards, the Canadian ambassador to Ireland, John Kearney, reported back to his government that after a visit to Joseph Walshe, he found the atmosphere in the Department of External Affairs 'profoundly depressed'. He said that Walshe 'even vaguely mooted some idea of an apology' and that it was evident 'the tide of public opinion was rising'.

However, that changed with the victory broadcast of Winston Churchill and his sharp criticism of Irish neutrality, in which he basically said 'Her Majesty's Government' would have been within its rights to 'come to close quarters with Mr de Valera'. And it would have been forced to do so without the 'loyalty and friendship of Northern Ireland'. De Valera's dignified response to these provocative remarks attracted enormous public support in Ireland for the Taoiseach and the call on Hempel was overshadowed, at least temporarily.

However, over the years, there has been regular criticism of de Valera's action. The possibility of the government apologising has also been raised. Some commentators have even suggested that de Valera may have been sympathetic to Nazi Germany – although all the evidence shows this was quite clearly not the case. De Valera had no sympathy for Hitler or the Nazis, but he clearly did have time for Edouard Hempel.

The discovery in recent times that the president of the day, Douglas Hyde, also expressed official condolences on the death of Hitler, has confirmed the belief that de Valera was simply following protocol. However, although his motives were honourable and he certainly cannot be accused of taking the easy option, it was unquestionably an error of judgment on the part of de Valera to do as he did.

Sixty years on, Minister for Justice Michael McDowell summed it up best when he said while the incident was very much of its time and de Valera did not intend to offer any insult to anybody, his call on Hempel was an exercise in 'excessive zeal' to protect Ireland's neutrality in the Second World War.

It is worth noting that years later state papers revealed that in the mid 1960s the Irish Jewish community funded the planting of a forest of 10,000 trees in Israel in honour of de Valera. He only agreed to the tribute on the understanding that it received no publicity.

James Dillon, who resigned from Fine Gael because he opposed neutrality and wanted Ireland to side with the allies, made an interesting – if at times contradictory – contribution in the Dáil that summer to de Valera's actions. He said he did not blame de Valera 'for carrying out the diplomatic minimum in expressing condolences to a state, the leader of which was dead'. However, he argued de Valera was 'unduly precipitate' for not, like Switzerland, waiting for an official notification of Hitler's death. Accusing de Valera of 'a gross and deplorable error of judgment', he said: 'There was no call on our people to perpetrate an act of supererogation in respect of the Nazi Reich. We were not offering condolences to a bereaved individual . . . The German Minister [ambassador] was not here as an individual, but as the representative of Nazism. Was it right for our Foreign Minister, in regard to that person, the representative of Nazism, to perpetrate an act of supererogation? I think it was not; I think it was a diplomatic blunder of the worst kind, and one that excited deep misunderstanding and great bitterness against us in circles where there would not be any bitterness if it had not been done.'

However, Dillon went on to say: 'I am certain that his Government as a whole hold no better brief for Nazism as a system than I hold – that is the truth . . . What is important is that the Taoiseach in doing what he did, was discharging only what he thought was the ordinary duty of diplomatic courtesy. If this House determined to remain neutral, one of the consequences was that we should treat the heads of every Government, German, American, British, French, Polish or otherwise, equally. We did that in our neutral position. I think we were wrong, but the Irish people thought we were right, and that is what matters, and, thinking they were right, they have no right to complain if their Minister carries out all the diplomatic implications of the policy which the Irish people have chosen to adopt.'

On Mature Recollection
Brian Lenihan

THE BACKGROUND

The year was 1990 and Ireland was getting ready for its first presidential election in almost two decades. The clear frontrunner was Brian Lenihan, Tanaiste in the Fianna Fáil/ Progressive Democrats coalition government and Minister for Defence. Hugely popular, with almost thirty years of cabinet experience, Lenihan had made a good recovery from a liver transplant operation and was expected to hold off the surprisingly strong challenge from the relatively unknown Labour candidate, Mary Robinson. After all, a Fianna Fáil candidate had never lost a presidential election.

But what would prove to be a very thorny issue was lurking in the background. Eight years earlier, on the night that Garret FitzGerald's Fine Gael government collapsed, calls had been made by Fianna Fáil to Áras an Uachtaráin in an unsuccessful attempt to put pressure on President Paddy Hillery not to dissolve the Dáil, thereby leaving the way clear for Charlie Haughey to form a government. It had always been presumed in political circles that Lenihan had been one of the people involved in making the calls to the Áras. This presumption had been widely reported and analysed in newspaper articles and books.

THE GAFFE

Just a couple of weeks before polling day, in an interview with the *Irish Press* newspaper and on RTÉ One's *Questions and Answers* programme, Lenihan insisted that he had played 'no hand, act or part' in efforts to pressurise the President. The problem for Lenihan was that months earlier, in an interview with post-graduate student Jim Duffy, Lenihan had spoken freely of how he had phoned the Áras on the night in question and spoken to the president.

THE IMPACT

When the tape recording of Lenihan's interview with Duffy was released on 25 October, 1990, not only was Lenihan's campaign thrown into turmoil, but the future of the FF/PD government was threatened.

Lenihan made matters worse by appearing on television on RTÉ One news and looking straight at the camera – in a manner described as Nixonesque by some commentators – pleading with the Irish people to believe him, arguing that 'on mature recollection', he had not phoned the Áras and his account to Duffy had been wrong. The term 'on mature recollection' immediately entered the political lexicon.

The Lenihan campaign was in free fall. A request for an audience with President Hillery to establish that Lenihan had not made the phone calls came to nothing. Fine Gael leader Alan Dukes moved to exploit the chaos within Fianna Fáil by putting down a motion of no confidence in the government. The move put immediate pressure on the PDs, who, because of the crisis, would have serious difficulties voting confidence in the government of which they were part. The smaller party decided it couldn't vote confidence in the government if Lenihan remained in the cabinet.

On 29 October, with the government on the verge of collapse, Haughey informed Lenihan that the PDs wanted him out and he bluntly told his Tanaiste to resign from government. Lenihan headed out on the campaign trail without giving any response and refused to take Haughey's calls. Emissaries from Haughey, including Bertie Ahern, were rebuffed. RTÉ's 9 o'clock news that night carried a report from the Lenihan campaign, stating that the Tanaiste would not be resigning from government. With the Dáil meeting the next day, it looked like the PD ministers were going to have to follow through on their threat to quit the government. However, faced with the prospect of a general election, in which Fianna Fáil would have been 'destroyed' (to quote Charlie McCreevy), Haughey told his long-time friend and political ally that he was ending his membership of the government. The move stopped the government from collapsing.

His dismissal from government prompted a wave of public sympathy for Lenihan and his poll rating recovered. However, comments from Padraig Flynn on RTÉ's *Saturday View* programme, claiming that Mary Robinson discovered a new interest in her family for the purpose of her presidential election campaign, (see Chapter 42), proved disastrous, effectively stalling the recovery.

In the election on 7 November, Lenihan topped the poll with 44% of the vote on the first count, ahead of Robinson with 39%. However, transfers from Fine Gael candidate Austin Currie gave Robinson an easy victory in the second count.

The whole incident caused enormous strains within government and led to huge resentment in Fianna Fáil towards the PDs.

For Lenihan, the controversy and the election defeat marked the end of his time as a major player in Irish politics, although he remained politically active up to his death in 1995 at the age of 64.

Mellow Yellow
Bertie Ahern

THE BACKGROUND

By June 2004, the boy from Drumcondra had really arrived. As president of the European Council, Bertie Ahern was enjoying being a player on the world stage and, what's more, he was proving to be pretty good at it. Ireland's presidency of the EU was coming to an end and it was widely accepted to be a massive success. When Ahern took over, there was deep pessimism within the EU about reaching agreement on key issues. By the end of his tenure, the Taoiseach had won admiration across Europe for his handling of the presidency, which would culminate in a deal on the EU constitution.

Ahern's stock was so high among the member states that the hugely prestigious job of President of the EU Commission was his for the taking if he had wanted it (the Taoiseach opted to stay in domestic politics instead). In the final month of the presidency, Ahern was invited to attend the G8 summit in his capacity as President of the European Council. There he would be rubbing shoulders with the leaders of the world's major industrialised countries.

THE GAFFE

The summit took place on Sea Island in Georgia, USA and the leaders were advised to dress down for a photo opportunity, involving a walk along the beach. The rest of the leaders basically just took off their ties. George Bush wore tweed, Silvio Berlusconi donned a typically stylish Italian suit, Gerhard Schroeder wore a black suit, while Tony Blair went for a classic Cary Grant-style casual ensemble of light jacket, crisp white shirt and dark trousers. However, standing out like a sore thumb in the pictures – beamed around the world – was the Taoiseach. Ahern committed an unspeakable crime against fashion by donning a beige jacket over a blue check shirt and, the *pièce de résistance*, a yellow pair of crumpled chino-style trousers. The look (or should that be 'don't look'?) was completed by a pair of brown shoes more appropriate for a formal suit – ouch!

THE IMPACT

Poor Bertie – or Bananaman as some newspapers dubbed him – was savaged. Brendan O'Connor described the look as 'Alan Whicker meets Colonel Saunders'. Top Irish designer Jen Kelly spoke for a nation when he described the outfit as 'vile', adding that it made him look like 'a banana split'.

'There he was among the world's leaders, looking like he wouldn't know whether his two shoes matched or not,' Kelly told the *Sunday Independent*. 'I was mortified to be Irish. He is missing Celia [Larkin, his former partner] by his side to say:

'Oh, no.' We all need a partner to keep us in line. I felt for him, he really got it wrong. We should all realise the seriousness of image on a global stage.'

Colour Me Beautiful director Joan Cashman said that Ahern looked like he was out walking the dog. 'The top half of the outfit was fine, his look could have been salvaged with a pair of dark trousers. He got one half of his outfit right and then lost the plot – it says he has lost the plot for Ireland too.'

Ahern buys most of his clothes from Louis Copeland menswear. The quality of the suits bought there helped him to dump the anorakman image of his early years in politics. Louis' brother and business partner Adrian Copeland told the *Sunday Independent* that the offending G8 outfit was from Louis Copeland's collection. 'He did get that from us, but not necessarily in that order,' he said. 'Normally we would suggest a pair of denim blue trousers with that jacket, but good old Bertie gets his colours completely askew when he is let loose. He shouldn't have been let out in that outfit.'

Copeland continued: 'Most of Bertie's stuff comes from us and 95 percent of the time he is properly attired. But we are willing to take the criticism as well. We know Bertie well and he likes his checked casual look. Please God he will start getting into stripes instead. The quality of our clothes is so good that it lasts for ages and the outfit Bertie wore was one he would have had for a while. He suits a more structured look, but there are times that call for less structure. We will be slagging him about this week's wardrobe, but he'll take it well. He is long past worrying what people say about his dress-sense. But some people really shouldn't be let dress themselves.'

It was left to Ahern's ex-wife Miriam to bring a sense of proportion to the whole thing. 'I think people are too pass-remarkable about other's clothes,' she was quoted as saying. 'I mean, it hardly matters that much.'

However, even in the serious environment of Dáil Éireann, the Taoiseach couldn't escape the fallout from his choice of outfit on Sea Island. 'The Taoiseach recently returned from the G8 Summit, at which his sartorial choice generated more publicity than the economic proposals made at the meeting,' Fine Gael leader Enda Kenny said. Labour leader Pat Rabbitte joined in suggesting the Taoiseach had lost out on the job of European Commission president as a result of his unfortunate choice of outfit. 'When Schroeder saw the gear, that is what did it. The Taoiseach had it up to then. He had it in the bag'. Ahern gamely responded: 'He liked it. I had to add some colour'.

The outfit was noted outside Ireland too. When RTÉ's Washington DC correspondent Carole Coleman interviewed US President George Bush as part of his visit to Ireland, the presidential staff reportedly suggested to Coleman that she ask him a question on the outfit that Ahern wore to the G8 summit. Coleman sensibly opted to ask her own questions.

Speaking about the fashion *faux-pas* two years later on RTÉ One's *Tubridy Tonight* show, Ahern was happy to poke fun at himself. To laughter from the audience, Ahern said: 'I was there with Putin, Chirac and Bush, so I had no chance. I had to stand out some way. Now everyone remembers the jacket and no-one remembers the meeting.' Everyone it seems except the Taoiseach.

It was the trousers, not the jacket, that were yellow, Bertie.

Mother Mary
Padraig Flynn

THE BACKGROUND

The 1990 presidential election was entering its final week. The election was turned on its head when the frontrunner, then Tanaiste Brian Lenihan, became involved in a controversy that sent his campaign into a major tailspin. Lenihan denied on television that on the night Garret FitzGerald's government fell eight years earlier, he (Lenihan) had put pressure on President Patrick Hillery not to dissolve the Dáil.

The problem for Lenihan was that he had already given an interview to a post-graduate student, Jim Duffy, in which he spoke about how he had phoned Áras an Uachtaráin on that night and spoken to the president (see Chapter 40). The revelation immediately threatened the future of the Fianna Fáil/Progressive Democrats coalition, a crisis that was only averted when Taoiseach Charlie Haughey fired Lenihan from the cabinet. While the revelations in the Jim Duffy interview had seriously damaged Lenihan's standing in the opinion polls, there was a major wave of public sympathy and an increase in support for him after he was sacked. It appeared, briefly, that he might be able to hold off the formidable challenge of Labour's candidate Mary Robinson. However, public opinion was about to be dramatically influenced once more. During RTÉ Radio One's *Saturday View* radio programme, Environment Minister Padraig Flynn made comments about Robinson that effectively ensured that Ireland would have its first woman president.

THE GAFFE

Flynn suggested on radio that Robinson had remodelled her image for the campaign, stating she had discovered a 'new interest in her family, being a mother and all that kind of thing, but . . . none of us who knew Mrs Robinson very well in previous incarnations ever heard her claiming to be a great wife and mother'.

The remarks were bad enough to begin with but any hope that they might have slipped under the political radar were quickly dashed when Michael McDowell, also a guest on the radio programme, pounced on the remarks, branding them disgusting and demanding they be withdrawn immediately. In the ensuing furore, Flynn did apologise, but only after the Taoiseach forced him to do so.

THE IMPACT

The consequences for Lenihan's campaign and, in the longer term, for Flynn personally were enormous. The immediate

result of the comments was to cut off the flow of public sympathy for Lenihan after his sacking. While the former Tanaiste would still top the poll on the first count, transfers from Fine Gael candidate Austin Currie gave Robinson a comfortable victory on the second count. Robinson's victory was to change the role of the president in Irish life forever, but who knows what would have happened had Flynn not made that critical intervention.

For Flynn, the comments cemented his status as a hate figure for the liberal left and probably marked the beginning of the end of his career in domestic politics. The hugely popular radio satire show *Scrap Saturday* hilariously lampooned him as Pee Flynnstone – 'Get away Wilma, what would you know, you're only a stupid woman'.

Just over a year later, Flynn was a key player as Albert Reynolds took over as leader of Fianna Fáil and Taoiseach. But the major influence he held in the Reynolds government would be short-lived. After the 1992 general election, a triumphant Labour Party – building on the success of the Robinson presidential campaign – was calling the shots. While it surprisingly and controversially opted to go into government with Fianna Fáil, Labour made it clear that it wouldn't countenance Flynn being a part of the cabinet.

The Mayoman departed to Brussels to become Ireland's new EU Commissioner. It is widely accepted that he did a good job in Brussels but, alas for Flynn, he didn't learn his lesson from his *Saturday View* faux pas and returned in 1999 for another broadcasting 'tour de farce', creating yet more controversy for him and his party (see Chapter 12).

The Thundering Disgrace

Paddy Donegan

THE BACKGROUND

In July 1976, the British ambassador to Ireland, Christopher Ewart-Biggs, was murdered by the IRA. The Fine Gael-Labour governing coalition responded to demands for anti-terrorist measures with the Emergency Powers Bill, allowing terrorist suspects to be detained for up to seven days without charge. However, President Cearbhall O'Dálaigh exercised his right to refer the controversial bill to the Supreme Court to test its constitutionality.

THE GAFFE

Defence Minister Paddy Donegan attended a ceremony in Columb Barracks, Mullingar on 18 October, 1976. In a speech, he attacked O'Dálaigh's decision stating: 'In my opinion, he is a thundering disgrace. The fact is that the army must stand behind the state.'

THE IMPACT

Seismic, resulting in the resignation of a president and, in retrospect, arguably finishing the coalition's chance of being re-elected in the following year's general election. The infamous comments sparked a constitutional crisis. O'Dálaigh, as president, was the nominal head of the defence forces and Donegan, as Defence Minister, had received his seal of office from him. While the two words 'thundering disgrace' are best remembered, the comment about the army standing 'behind the state' particularly angered O'Dálaigh, who interpreted it as being a suggestion that he, as commander-in-chief of the Irish army, didn't stand behind the state.

Donegan offered to resign from the cabinet, but Taoiseach Liam Cosgrave refused the offer and defended his minister in the Dáil when Fianna Fail introduced a motion calling for him to resign. That motion was defeated. The Louth TD also sought to meet with O'Dálaigh to apologise but the president refused to meet him. Donegan did issue a statement stating his remarks 'arose out of my deep feelings for the security of our citizens. I intend to offer my apologies to the President as soon as possible.'

However, with Donegan staying on as Minister, O'Dálaigh, a former chief justice and attorney general, felt he had no option but to resign, declaring 'this was the only way open to assert publicly my personal integrity and independence as President of Ireland, and to protect the dignity and independence of the Presidency as an institution'. He was replaced as president by Fianna Fáil Minister Paddy Hillery.

The Donegan affair was a public relations disaster for the government. A few months later, Donegan was effectively demoted to Minister for Lands in a cabinet reshuffle.

The following year, the coalition was annihilated in the general election as Fianna Fáil swept back to power with a 20 seat Dáil majority. In an interview that year with *The Irish Times*, Donegan said he had been suffering from the effects of a severe car accident on the previous night when he made his Mullingar remarks. 'I was concussed and did not know it. I was like a zombie walking around.'

Although he had two whiskies at a reception before the meal, Donegan was adamant in the interview that there was no question of drink being solely behind his remarks. It has long been rumoured that Donegan's outburst was a lot more colourful and that the version published in the media was a sanitised one. It was suggested in some quarters that the actual words used were 'f**king b*****ks and a thundering disgrace'. However, the one journalist present at the occasion has always dismissed this, stating that the actual words used were 'thundering disgrace' and nothing else.

Richard Goebbels?

Michael McDowell

THE BACKGROUND

March 2006 and Fine Gael's Finance spokesman and Dublin North Central TD Richard Bruton issued a statement that Garda numbers in the Dublin Metropolitian Area had increased by just two in 2005. Bruton was basing his claim on figures released to him by Justice Minister Michael McDowell in response to a parliamentary question. It was normal political knock-about stuff that would hardly have attracted any public attention.

THE GAFFE

At an impromptu press conference outside Buswell's Hotel, opposite Leinster House, McDowell very publicly 'lost it'. Visibly angry, he dismissed Bruton's statements and went on to compare Bruton – one of the most even tempered and polite members of the Dáil – to Nazi propagandist Joseph Goebbels. 'He is, I believe, the Dr Goebbels of propaganda and the figures I am issuing here today prove conclusively that what he is saying is rubbish.'

The Minister then waved a piece of paper at journalists which he said showed that Garda numbers had increased in Dublin by 278 since he arrived at the Department of Justice in 2002, and that Bruton had 'suppressed' other figures which showed this.

'The facts are he has manipulated public opinion in a disgraceful way and I am going to call on him. Go into the Dáil, put down a motion. Square up to me man to man on this issue and I will win the debate hands down. I'm really angry with him and I think that it's about time that he got out of his ivory tower. He resembles a kind of post-graduate student floating around that house [Dáil] over there.'

He added that Bruton had used 'selective figures to prove a falsehood . . . Deputy Bruton is knee-high to me in terms of anything that he ever managed to do for this country.'

THE IMPACT

It was a PR disaster for the Justice Minister. To lose his cool over such a small issue raised questions about his judgment, while to compare the popular and respected Bruton with a Nazi propagandist was seen as way over the top. It didn't help that the Minister had recently made what were seen as outrageous and unwarranted comments during a row with constituency rival and Green Party TD John Gormley, appearing to draw a link between the Green Party and those involved in the Dublin riots of a few weeks earlier. These comments were regarded as having no substance whatsoever.

The next morning, accepting the old political adage to 'stop digging when you are in a hole', a chastened McDowell went on RTÉ Radio One's *Morning Ireland* to apologise publicly to Bruton.

'I do regret saying that, and I was playing the man and not the ball. And I do apologise unreservedly to Richard Bruton for calling him the Joseph Goebbels of propaganda. It was over the top, it was intemperate and I was being thin-skinned.'

McDowell said he made the outburst because he was annoyed at Bruton. 'I was angry because during the period that I have been Minister for Justice the number of gardaí attached to the Dublin Metropolitan District have gone up by 270. I know and like Richard Bruton and I don't think he's the Goebbels of propaganda. He made a point which, if I had gotten the same statistic out of a PQ [parliamentary question] I'd be tempted to use it myself.'

Stressing he had not been urged by anyone else in the cabinet to apologise, the Minister added: 'I am big enough to admit I have made a mistake . . . It's very much off my own bat. I had a slightly sleepless night.' McDowell later buttressed the apology by shaking hands with Bruton in the Dáil chamber.

On the same day, McDowell withdrew the remarks he had made two weeks earlier about the Greens.

Commenting the next day, in an editorial *The Irish Times* said that the Minister 'overstepped the mark by engaging in vulgar personal abuse, arrogant behaviour and downright misrepresentation in seeking to deflect attention from the inadequacies of the policing system for which he is responsible. It was a tawdry episode that will damage his image and raise questions over the credibility of his future pronouncements. The only saving aspect of the contretemps was the comprehensive apology he tendered to Richard Bruton.'

The apology did have the effect of taking the heat out of the story and while government figures accepted that having to make two apologies in one day was 'one too many', few believed the damage to McDowell would be long term.

Flu Jab Ferris

Martin Ferris

THE BACKGROUND

In the general election of May 2002, Sinn Féin made major electoral gains, increasing their seat total from one to five. One of the four first time TDs was Kerry North's Martin Ferris. Ferris, who spent ten years in jail for attempting to smuggle in weaponry for the IRA, took a seat at the expense of former Tanaiste Dick Spring.

THE GAFFE

Later that year, despite earning a TD's salary of €71,800 plus substantial expenses, Ferris used a medical card for a flu vaccination instead of paying for it himself.

THE IMPACT

The story soon emerged in the *Sunday World* which labelled him a 'scrounger' for using the medical card scheme while earning such a large salary at a time when many deserving families were denied cards.

Ferris worked full-time for Sinn Féin in Kerry North for several years before the 2002 general election. However, Sinn Féin insisted he was not financially supported by the party during that time. The Southern Health Board confirmed that Ferris was entitled to the medical card and would remain so until May 2005. Under a 1996 back-to-work scheme, the long-term unemployed are entitled to retain medical cards for three years after they get a job.

Ferris was technically in the right. However, given the size of his new salary, the story was a major embarrassment for Sinn Féin, which had been assiduously courting the working-class vote across the country. Fine Gael's health spokeswoman Olivia Mitchell immediately accused the Kerry TD of 'abusing' the system.

Sinn Féin quickly went into damage limitation mode. Ferris claimed he intended not to renew his card when it expired at the end of 2002 and would instead join the VHI. 'When I came out of prison, I had not worked in 10 years and had no income. So I was entitled to a medical card,' he said.

The day after the story broke, a spokesperson for Sinn Féin conceded that Ferris had been 'politically naïve' to hold on to a medical card after his election to the Dáil.

'Maybe there has been a misjudgment here on his own part, but there is no doubt that he was entitled to it. He wasn't cheating, but it was possibly politically naïve for him not to realise that it would come out.'

Describing the *Sunday World*'s report as 'mischievous and inaccurate', a Sinn Féin statement said Mr Ferris, who suffers from severe asthma, would never have 'abused' the card.

Sinn Féin also stated that claims of Ferris earning €100,000 were rubbish. 'Deputy Ferris takes home the average industrial wage. A large proportion of his Dáil salary goes towards providing local constituency services and some also goes back to the party.'

With a general election four and a half years away at the time the story broke, the gaffe was never likely to have a long-term impact on Ferris and his electoral prospects. Given that controversies such as the Colombia Three and the Northern Bank robbery over the following years appeared to have little impact on Sinn Féin's standing in the polls, it was very unlikely that using a medical card to pay for a flu jab was going to cause lasting political damage to Ferris.

Noonan and his Merry Men

Fine Gael

THE BACKGROUND

In early 2001, Michael Noonan replaced John Bruton as leader of Fine Gael and Jim Mitchell became deputy leader. The Noonan/Mitchell ticket was immediately dubbed the 'dream team', but despite the two men's obvious abilities, it failed to grab the imagination of the electorate. With public and private polls pointing to a comfortable Fianna Fáil victory in the 2002 general election, Fine Gael was under serious pressure to come up with new, innovative policies. The 1999 flotation of Telecom Eireann (which later became Eircom) was seen as a potential weak spot for the government because many small investors had lost money as the share price failed to continue its initial rise.

THE GAFFE

In early 2002, four months before the general election, Fine Gael's front bench agreed to a radical proposal to compensate those who had lost money on their Eircom shares. If elected, the party would allow 400,000 taxpayers to recoup 20% of their Eircom losses by offsetting them against their annual tax bill.

THE IMPACT

Presumably, somebody in Fine Gael thought the party had hit on a winning formula. The white knights of Fine Gael would ride in to rescue the tens of thousands of small investors who had lost money on Eircom shares because the big bad government had priced the stock too high at flotation. In true Robin Hood style, Fine Gael would return up to €90 million to beleaguered investors and the gratitude of the electorate would be endless. Boy, was he or she wrong! The proposal went down as badly as the Eircom share price.

The backlash was instantaneous. It's hard to know why some ideas grab the public imagination and others are derided. Rightly or wrongly, this proposal was regarded as a naked vote-grabbing exercise that would set a dangerous precedent, leading people to believe there would be a safety net for them if they invested in the stock market.

A gleeful government turned the big guns on Fine Gael. Taoiseach Bertie Ahern said the proposal couldn't work because it would create a number of tax anomalies. Tanaiste Mary Harney said the measure would set 'a very dangerous precedent', noting: 'When we invest in stocks and shares we take on board all of the risks involved.'

Finance Minister Charlie McCreevy was more scathing, claiming the proposal was tantamount to suggesting that people should receive tax relief for losing money at the races. 'You can

go back over the last 20 years and come up with ridiculous ideas we all came up with, including myself. Fine Gael doesn't have a monopoly on ridiculous ideas but this one is in the premier league of such ideas.' Even Labour Party sources privately expressed doubts that the measure could work.

Michael Noonan went on RTÉ's *Liveline* programme to defend the proposal saying it would compensate people 'conned' into buying shares by the government, which had hyped the share offer 'through a very expensive public relations campaign'.

'I don't think a single shareholder who got burned in Eircom will buy a share in a State company again unless something is done, so as a matter of national policy as well as compensation, I think it's very important to restore confidence,' he said.

Arguing this was aimed at 'the small person', Noonan argued: 'What's sauce for the goose is sauce for the gander and if the big men can offset it against capital gains at 20 per cent, I can't see why the small man and woman can't offset it against tax'.

While Noonan certainly had a point about the big investors being able to offset their losses, it never got properly aired and there is no question that the proposal backfired massively on Fine Gael.

It's impossible to know how much of Fine Gael's subsequent electoral collapse – the party lost 23 seats in the May 2002 general election – can be put down to this proposal. There were many reasons for that disastrous performance. With hindsight, Fine Gael was not going to win that election regardless of what it did. But what can be said is that the Eircom shareholders' proposal – along with a subsequent promise to compensate taxi drivers who had lost out under deregulation – seriously undermined the party's credibility with an election just a few short months away.

Willie the Kid

Willie O'Dea

THE BACKGROUND

In November 2005, Defence Minister Willie O'Dea visited the Curragh Camp in Kildare to mark the 25th anniversary of the establishment of the Army Ranger Wing – the elite special forces unit in the Defence Forces. During the visit, the Minister inspected weaponry and other equipment used by the Ranger Wing.

THE GAFFE

The Minister allowed himself to be photographed with an automatic pistol in his hand pointing straight at the camera. The photograph of the smiling minister was widely published, making page one of *The Irish Times* the day after his visit. The timing of the photograph was particularly unfortunate because the issue of crime gangs in Dublin and the growing gun culture was a really hot topic in the news at this time.

THE IMPACT

The impact was largely short-lived, but the incident produced no shortage of indignation and outrage at the time. Opposition parties jumped all over the Minister. Labour leader Pat Rabbitte described it as an 'ill-judged tasteless stunt by a Minister mad on publicity'. He accused O'Dea of making guns a 'matter of frivolity at a time when two warring gangs are feuding and risking public safety on the streets of this city' [Dublin].

Green Party leader Trevor Sargent also raised the issue in the Dáil. He went so far as to accuse the government of promoting gun culture through the photograph. He demanded – but was ruled out of order – a special debate to 'allow the Minister for Defence to explain why he allowed himself to be photographed pointing a gun at a cameraman, and to hear the government policy on how it can reconcile this promotion of a gun culture with the horrific shootings and escalating levels of violent crime occurring on a day-to-day basis'.

Socialist Party TD Joe Higgins probably struck a more appropriate note with his humerous dig at the Minister. Higgins prompted huge laughter in the Dáil when he asked Tanaiste Mary Harney: 'Did you as a matter of Dáil security at least require the Minister to leave his weapon at the door this morning?'

Top marks also for Fine Gael's Jim O'Keeffe who asked if the Minister would now be known as 'Willie the Kid?'

In response, a contrite O'Dea told RTÉ that he did not mean to offend anyone by posing for the photo. He said it would be wrong for anyone to think the picture indicated that he or the government wished to glamorise gun crime. 'I would regret it if people's sensibilities were affected, or if they were led to those conclusions. That is certainly not what I intended,' he said.

O'Dea stressed the pistol was unloaded and that he had handled it under military supervision. Photographers had asked him to hold up the weapon when he had been examining it.

'All the weapons I handled yesterday were unloaded and rendered harmless. There's no question about that. I hope nobody is of the opinion that the gun was loaded in any way,' he said.

He also undertook not to pose for such a picture again. 'There was a lot of photographers around, they took literally dozens, if not hundreds, of photographs as I looked at various weapons and various pieces of equipment. On various occasions the photographers asked me to look up and hold it up here, you know, what usually happens . . . Out of all the photographs taken, this was the one they used.'

However, he also couldn't resist taking aim at Pat Rabbitte for his comments in the Dáil. The Labour leader, O'Dea said, would some day 'drown in his own pomposity'. 'He seems to be permanently in awe at his own cleverness. Now he is permanently in awe of his own pomposity . . . I mean my message to Pat Rabbitte is quite simply, get a life.'

Enda KenYa

Enda Kenny

THE BACKGROUND

It was June 2006 and with less than twelve months to go to an election, Enda Kenny had succeeded in turning Fine Gael from no-hopers to genuine contenders. Fine Gael had traditionally been the party of law and order and Kenny was successfully rebuilding that image with strong attacks on the level of crime under the Fianna Fáil/Progressive Democrats government. A 'tough on crime' speech by Kenny at the party's Ard Fheis had been well received.

While the party's no-nonsense approach was dismissed as simplistic and over-the-top by some commentators, it seemed to be popular with voters and was regarded as a major factor in the party's steady rise in support in opinion polls. Building on this image, the party sought to introduce a controversial Home Defence Bill, which would allow homeowners to use reasonable force to defend their property and family.

THE GAFFE

During the debate in the Dáil on the bill, Kenny declared: 'This Bill only applies in the case of an intruder breaking into the home. I do not know if the minister [for Justice Michael McDowell] has ever been attacked. I was mugged once by two people, high on drugs, with a knife, which was a pretty daunting prospect.' He added: 'Until the day I die, I will remember the rasping sound of a knife being pulled from a leather scabbard and the impression that leaves on one's mind. For me, it was not a case of fear but of being prepared to fight for my life, literally.'

The problem for Kenny was that having heard this impassioned and highly moving tale, the media was hungry for more detail. Queries were quickly lodged with Fine Gael's press office: Where and when had the mugging happened? Had Kenny reported the matter to the Gardaí? The latter point was particularly crucial given that the Fine Gael leader was anxious to stress his law and order credentials. But checks with the Gardaí revealed that no such incident had ever been reported in Kenny's home county of Mayo.

Journalists were not put off by the party's stonewalling that it was a private matter. Private matters cease being private when the person involved raises them in a Dáil debate to score political points against his opponent. Eventually, after a day of persistent questioning by journalists, the truth came out: the incident happened not on the mean streets of Dublin or in the more benign environs of Castlebar, but in Kenya, 12 years earlier when Kenny was holidaying there. Kenny had apparently been alone when confronted by two would-be attackers. Though there had been no physical entanglement,

Kenny had privately told people that the terrifying incident had 'stayed with me' and that he could 'still picture the exact moment' of the confrontation.

THE IMPACT

While the story proved something of a two-day wonder, it was still a major embarrassment for Kenny. The general view, rightly or wrongly, was that Kenny had given the clear implication that the incident had happened in Ireland. He faced immediate accusations of 'cynically spinning the story to whip up fear for political gain' and of being 'at best disingenuous and incomplete and at worst, deliberately evasive and misleading'. RTÉ's hugely influential phone-in show *Liveline* devoted a programme to the story, while the Irish edition of *The Daily Mail* splashed the headline – 'Truth about Kenny's mugging (It was in Kenya . . . twelve years ago)' – across its front page.

The paper quoted Fianna Fáil TD Martin Brady as saying: 'If he wanted to tell the story at all, he should have told the whole story in the first place. Now we hear Enda was mugged in Kenya in 1994? Now that's unfortunate, and I feel sorry for his trouble, but it's hardly relevant to a debate on legislation in Ireland in 2006. It's a bit rich and a bit sad, if you ask me.'

Another Fianna Fáil TD, deputy chief whip Billy Kelleher, said Kenny was guilty of whipping up fears and of trying 'to pull the wool over everyone's eyes with his half-true tale' of being attacked. 'He misled the Dáil during a debate on crime with a story that's 12 years old and happened half a world away,' Kelleher said. 'You have to hand it to Enda for embellishment, though. His account of an attack at knife-point was certainly moving – only it didn't happen in Ireland. Can we really trust this man in Government?'

And Dublin Mid-West TD John Curran said that Kenny's reluctance to come clean about the location and date of his mugging showed he was happy to give the false impression that the crime happened in Ireland. 'This is the latest attempt by Fine Gael to damage the reputation of Dublin and give the impression we are all living in Dodge City,' Curran said. He added that while there were genuine concerns about crime in Dublin, Kenny and his party were 'happy to go completely over the top and give Dublin the reputation of being the crime capital of Europe where people are fearful of venturing outdoors'.

The Daily Mail did some research on Kenny's claim that there was a 'rasping' noise as the knife was withdrawn from its leather scabbard. 'The muggers of Nairobi,' the newspaper revealed, 'would normally conceal a weapon on their clothing and, experts say, a knife would not make a rasping sound when taken from a leather sheath.'

E-mails also flew about with an image from Kenny's recent highly effective 'I'll make criminals pay for their crimes' poster, but with the words 'in Kenya' tagged on.

The Wrong Road

Jim McDaid

THE BACKGROUND

In the autumn of 2004, Donegal TD Jim McDaid returned to the backbenches having lost out in a reshuffle of junior ministers. Before that, he had been responsible for road traffic as Minister of State for Transport. In that role, he spearheaded the government's anti drink-driving campaign. At the launch of that campaign he had warned: 'Some drivers still choose to ignore our drink-driving laws and as a result innocent lives are destroyed.' In July 2004, at an Institute of Road Safety conference, he noted that 'significant levels of speeding, drink-driving and non-compliance with seat-belt wearing still exists'.

THE GAFFE

On 26 April, 2005, McDaid spent a day at the races in Punchestown. While there, he drank up to seven glasses of wine and then got into his car at the Citywest Hotel on the outskirts of Dublin. According to a front-page report in the *Irish Independent* when the story broke two days later, McDaid 'drunkenly drove up the wrong side of a busy dual carriageway before a concerned haulier brought a madcap chase to a safe end'. It reported that McDaid was 'then arrested by a plainclothes garda who had also joined the pursuit'.

The report explained that McDaid drove down the N7 away from Dublin, whereupon he turned left onto a slip road, heading for Newbridge. He then came to Newhall roundabout, but turned right and drove the wrong way around the roundabout before continuing up the wrong side of the dual carriageway, known as the Newbridge Road. 'Other vehicles, which met the TD's brand new Volvo, were seen swerving to avoid the car,' the report said, adding that the haulier was 'able to get to the Togher roundabout in advance of the TD and used his truck to block two lanes and halt the car's progress.' The former minister was taken to Naas Garda station and was later found to have been more than three times over the legal alcohol limit.

THE IMPACT

The incident was a personal nightmare for McDaid, although there was the considerable consolation that nobody had been killed or injured. Not surprisingly, the incident attracted enormous publicity. Friends of McDaid said he was genuinely devastated and hugely remorseful over what he had done. Nor, to be fair, did McDaid try and hide behind any legal protection, with a court action pending. He accepted that as a public representative, he had a particular obligation to uphold the law and issued a brief statement saying he wished to 'unreservedly apologise for my serious lapse in behaviour last night. It was completely wrong of me to drive a car while under the influence of drink. This will now be a matter for the Gardaí to deal with.'

The following October, in Naas District Court, McDaid was fined €750 and disqualified from driving for two years after being convicted of drink-driving and dangerous driving. The court heard that analysis of a blood sample taken showed 267 milligrams of alcohol per 100 millilitres of blood. The legal limit is 80 milligrams of alcohol per 100 millilitres of blood.

In a statement read to the court, McDaid said he had no excuse for his actions. 'For me to get behind the wheel of a motor vehicle in my condition was a disgrace. It is something that I will never forget or indeed, regretfully, never be allowed to forget,' he said. Judge Murrough Connellan said it was extremely lucky that no one had been injured in the incident.

Speaking to reporters afterwards, McDaid said he had been called a disgrace and an idiot for what he had done and he accepted these descriptions as quite right. His actions were 'all the worse' given that he had fronted an anti-drink driving campaign while Junior Minister at the Department of Transport. McDaid's solicitor Brian Price said that on the morning of the incident his client had left Donegal extremely early without eating breakfast, as he was due to undergo a dental procedure that required an anaesthetic. McDaid returned to Leinster House after the dental operation. Feeling nauseous, he had gone to his office rather than to have something to eat. The court heard that later in the day, McDaid had decided to go to Punchestown Races, after receiving an invite from a friend. He drove to Citywest Hotel where he was picked up and taken to the racecourse. Price said that up to 4.00pm his client drank only water, but that later he was invited to a corporate box, where he drank between five and seven glasses of wine.

When he returned to the Citywest Hotel, McDaid took a taxi back to his hotel in the city. However, he remembered that his change of clothes and toiletries were in his car at the hotel and he asked the taxi to turn around. McDaid then made a 'tragic mistake', Price said, in deciding to drive his own car back to Dublin. He said that on leaving the hotel, McDaid had mistakenly driven south rather than north towards Dublin.

It seems beyond question that had McDaid still been a minister when the incident happened, his position would have been untenable. As it was, questions were raised about whether he would continue in politics. McDaid told reporters on the day of the court case that he had not decided on his political future and whether he would stand again at the next general election.

The following April, 12 months after he was arrested driving from Citywest, McDaid announced that he would be retiring from public life at the following general election. Months later, he did a major u-turn and declared that he would, after all, contest the election. In a subsequent interview, McDaid described himself as an alcoholic who had a problem with binge drinking. He told the *Sunday Independent* he could go for long periods without drinking, but when he started, he found it difficult to 'put the cap back on the bottle'.

The Britshit PM

Persons unknown

THE BACKGROUND

It was November 1984 and no end was in sight to the Troubles in Northern Ireland. The IRA ceasefire was still a decade away and relations between the Irish and British governments were in the doldrums. There was fury in Ireland as Margaret Thatcher emerged from a summit meeting with Taoiseach Garret FitzGerald on 19 November and gave her infamous 'out, out, out' dismissal of the three options presented by the New Ireland Forum. To quote: '. . . a united Ireland was one solution. That is out. A second solution was confederation of the two states. That is out. A third solution was joint authority. That is out.' Her comments were considered by nationalists as being totally dismissive.

Two days later it was reported that FitzGerald told a Fine Gael party meeting that Thatcher's behaviour during the press conference had been 'gratuitously offensive'. Some years later, writing in his autobiography, FitzGerald argued that he was commenting on the fact that he '. . . recognised that her remarks were seen as gratuitously offensive'. Either way, emotions were running high.

The day after the summit press conference, FitzGerald and Fianna Fáil leader Charlie Haughey had a heated debate in the Dáil over whether Thatcher referred to the 'equal respect due to these two identities' in Northern Ireland during the press conference. FitzGerald maintained she had, Haughey insisted she had actually done 'the opposite' and accused the Taoiseach of misleading the house. At one point, FitzGerald told Haughey to read the transcript of the press conference, adding: 'The Deputy should not speak from ignorance.' Haughey replied: 'That is a lie. That is not what the British Prime Minister said.' The Leas-Cheann Comhairle asked Haughey to 'withdraw that remark', which the opposition leader duly did.

THE GAFFE

When the unrevised official edition of the Dáil debates for 20 November was published some days later – this was long before the Internet and next-day access to debates on the web – a misprint was discovered. According to the text, Haughey referred not to 'the British Prime Minister' but, to the 'Britshit Prime Minister'. The typographical error was compounded by the fact that the Leas-Cheann Comhairle had asked Haughey to 'withdraw that remark'. While the Leas-Cheann Comhairle had been referring to the use of the word 'lie', for those reading the incorrect official edition, it looked as if he was asking Haughey to withdraw the description 'Britshit'.

THE IMPACT

Much tee-heeing all round, although hundreds of copies of the edition had to be withdrawn and sent for correction. A government spokesman confirmed to the media that the clerk of the Dáil had requested the return of the copies and that only a handful had been sold in the Government Publications Office – which presumably became collectors' items.

A spokesman for Fianna Fáil was quoted as saying: 'Our view on it is that this was a printer's error contained in the unrevised report of the Dáil proceedings. As we understand it, this error was spotted by the staff of the House and the copies were withdrawn. It was very obviously a mistake.' Very obviously, although such was the antipathy towards Mrs Thatcher in Ireland at that time, many people might have concurred with the misprint.

Ironically, some copies of the official edition of the Dáil debates were sent at the time to the House of Commons, although presumably it is the corrected version that is located there today.

Char-Li's Sidestep

Charlie Haughey

THE BACKGROUND

It was Autumn 1991 and once again the Taoiseach of the day, Charlie Haughey, was in trouble. A series of controversies in the semi-state sector – most notably in the newly privatised Telecom Eireann and the newly privatised Greencore Food Group – and in the beef industry had sent his government into a tailspin. The sense of dismay and worry within Fianna Fáil at Haughey's handling of the controversies only added to concerns raised by the party's poor performance in the local elections of the previous June.

After four years of generally positive reviews of the government's economic performance, the economy – largely due to international factors – had dipped. Overall, the outlook was gloomy. In late September, Haughey was scheduled to do a state-of-the-nation type interview with RTÉ Radio One's flagship show *This Week*. The day before the interview, Haughey held a 'council of war' at his home in Kinsealy, where a strategy was developed. Haughey would use the interview to calm the growing political storm and be seen to once again take charge of the situation.

THE GAFFE

What was later dubbed the 'step aside plan' was a key component of the strategy. During the interview with presenter Sean O'Rourke, Haughey said two chairmen of state bodies – Michael Smurfit, chairman of Telecom Eireann, and Seamus Pairceir, chairman of the Custom House Docks Development Authority – should 'step aside' or temporarily vacate their chairs until an inquiry into the Telecom Eireann purchase of the Johnston Mooney & O'Brien site was complete.

It was speculated afterwards that the two men were not told of Haughey's plan in advance so they would not be able to resign prior to the interview. Smurfit was an investor in United Property Holdings (UPH), the property company set up by NCB which originally purchased the Johnston Mooney & O'Brien site in November 1988. UPH, the following year, sold it to a company called Chestvale, which in turn sold the site to Telecom. The Inspector's report into the affair later found that Smurfit had no financial interest in the sale, other than his shares in UPH. Pairceir – a former chairman of the Revenue Commissioners – was chairman of UPH, but his role was strictly non-executive. Haughey's call for these two men to step aside infuriated a number of Fianna Fáil TDs.

During the interview, Haughey also stated that it was his intention to lead Fianna Fáil into the next election. He joked that 'some of these Chinese leaders go on til they are eighty or ninety, but I think that's probably a bit long'.

THE IMPACT

Far from defusing the situation, the interview actually hardened views that it might be time for Haughey to step aside and it directly precipitated a leadership heave. Firstly, the Chinese leaders joke seriously backfired. The political editor of the *Irish Independent* Chris Glennon, described it as 'the joke that went wrong', writing that it 'sent a shudder down many a Fianna Fáil spine, especially as he also indicated that reshuffles were not really part of the government scene here and that ministers of state would not be sacked to make room for young tigers'. Haughey had to backtrack. A few weeks later, in an emotional speech to Fianna Fáil TDs, he told them he would know when it was time to go – the clear implication being that he would complete his agenda and step down.

The 'step aside plan' also failed to have the desired effect. Both Pairceir and Smurfit were, not surprisingly, furious with what Haughey had done. Pairceir was actually on his way to Belfast, where he was to represent the Docks Development Authority, when he heard his position being undermined by Haughey on the radio. He immediately turned his car around and drove back to Dublin, where he let it be known that he had no option but to resign – not step aside. 'There are some things that are just too much to take,' he said. Smurfit followed suit, making it clear that talk of stepping aside was 'unrealistic' and stressing that he had acted properly at all times during his 12-year association with Telecom and that he 'deeply resented any suggestions to the contrary'.

Pat Cox, an MEP for the Progressive Democrats, who were Fianna Fáil's coalition partner was asked if the resignations meant an end of the pressure on the government. He didn't prevaricate: 'Absolutely not,' he said. The spotlight was quickly back on the Taoiseach and his perceived dithering of the previous month. Glennon wrote in the *Irish Independent* that 'his best effort on the Telecom Affair – the 'Step aside plan' – left him like a bomb disposal expert who cut the wrong wire and set off an explosion'.

In the same newspaper, Bruce Arnold accused Haughey of 'distancing himself from trouble, taking no responsibility for the shame and humiliation felt by his party, and resorting to the cutting off and punishment of others as a device for saving himself'. Arnold argued that Haughey, a very experienced politician, must have recognised the 'step aside' proposal was 'absurd' and 'how little it had to do with the problems, many of which derived from his own handling of power'.

The pressure piled on Haughey. An opinion poll showed plummeting ratings for him and his government. Just five days after the *This Week* interview was broadcast, four backbench TDs – Noel Dempsey, Liam Fitzgerald, MJ Nolan and Sean Power – came together with a public statement designed to increase the pressure on Haughey to step down. In the statement, they referred specifically to the *This Week* interview. 'We have watched with growing disquiet the events of the past three weeks in the semi-state sector. We fully endorse the actions of the relevant ministers in instituting full and wider ranging inquiries into these affairs . . . We are particularly concerned at the manner in which these matters were dealt with by an Taoiseach in his radio interview last week. We find it incomprehensible that the Taoiseach should suggest on air that someone of Seamus Pairceir's integrity should 'step aside', while he ignored the role of Mr Bernie Cahill, chairman of Greencore, in the sugar company affair.'

Just over a month later, one of the 'Gang of Four', Sean Power, put down a motion of no-confidence in Haughey. The Taoiseach survived that challenge but it was to prove a pyrrhic victory and a few short months later he had resigned as both Taoiseach and leader of Fianna Fáil. He was sixty-six when he bowed out – quite a bit younger than the eighty or ninety that his peers in China reached before retirement.

Robinson's Chile Handshake
Mary Robinson

THE BACKGROUND

In the 1990 presidential election, Mary Robinson sensationally beat the favourite Brian Lenihan, to wrestle the presidency away from Fianna Fáil for the first time in the State's history. She immediately raised the profile and expanded the role of the presidency and quickly became enormously popular with the general public. Reflecting this popularity, media coverage of the new president was overwhelmingly positive.

However, by 1995, there were clear signs that the honeymoon period with the media was over. Some newspapers had begun to criticise her around the time of her decision in 1993 to visit West Belfast and shake hands with Sinn Féin president Gerry Adams. There were also serious tensions emerging between the Áras and the Rainbow Government of Fine Gael, Labour and Democratic Left, particularly with Labour leader and Foreign Affairs Minister Dick Spring, who had championed Robinson's presidential campaign in 1990.

Spring and his cabinet colleagues felt that Robinson had

strayed into the political arena when she expressed fears about the genuine concerns of unionists in relation to the Framework Document – the seminal work published in February 1995 by the Irish and British governments which set out a joint vision of the future of Northern Ireland. On 19 March, 1995, Robinson set off on a two-week trip encompassing three state visits to Argentina, Chile and Brazil. As they were formal state visits, the host country largely called the shots, while the advance arrangements were left to the Irish ambassadors.

THE GAFFE

According to her authorised biography, written by Olivia O'Leary and Helen Burke, 'the President was roundly criticised for not meeting the poor, not seeing enough of the Irish community and finally for shaking the hand of Chile's notorious former dictator, General Pinochet'.

The first problem emerged in Argentina. The timing of the visit was unfortunate because there were impending elections and President Menem was understandably preoccupied after the death of his son. Because of the impending election, a visit to a poor area close to Buenos Aires where Irish Dominican nuns were based was ruled out by Menem – causing great disappointment to the nuns. Robinson later explained that her activities were constrained by the fact that it was a state visit, which meant she was a guest of the country that invited her and that if she could have met the Domincian nuns, 'you can be assured, I would have done so'. But this incident set the pattern for a trip that would be dogged by controversy.

It was the unsought encounter with Pinochet, a hate figure for the left worldwide for the way in which he ruthlessly repressed dissent as head of a military junta in Chile from 1973 to 1990, that will probably be best remembered. *The Irish Times* reported on 29 March, 1995, that Robinson 'gave a stiff frigid handshake to General Augusto Pinochet, the head of the Chilean armed forces, as she and President Eduardo Frei, greeted guests arriving for a state dinner in her honour in the presidential palace in Santiago'.

In her biography, O'Leary and Burke wrote: 'A human rights champion shaking hands with a dictator – this was the sort of publicity disaster that advance preparation could have avoided'. While this is undoubtedly true, to be fair to Robinson, she was put in an impossible situation on the night. As she later explained in an interview in *The Irish Times*, 'If you are a guest, you greet other guests and so I greeted him'. Asked how she felt about that, she said she could not express any personal view. The first she was aware that Pinochet would be attending the dinner in his capacity as head of the armed forces was when her highly regarded advisor, Bride Rosney, pulled her aside to warn her. *The Irish Times* reported that Chilean security officials 'clearly sensitive to the wishes of their visitor' ordered the RTÉ cameraman and soundman out of the reception room just before the general approached Robinson.

It should be pointed out that the president's 'stiff frigid handshake' was in contrast to the effusive greeting that Margaret Thatcher had previously given the former dictator. In her speech that night, Robinson pointedly welcomed with 'great satisfaction' the return of democratic structures and full freedom of expression in Chile. Pinochet, dressed in a white ceremonial jacket with five gold stars, listened impassively. The seating was arranged so the general did not sit with Robinson or with the Chilean Foreign Minister, Jose Miguel Insulza, who had been forced to spend a decade in exile during Pinochet's tenure. During after-dinner drinks, the Irish and Chilean presidents stayed in one room, while Pinochet stayed in another room and there was no conversation between the two parties.

Robinson later told her biographers: 'We genuinely didn't know he would be there. We were absolutely amazed. Bride was flabbergasted.' However, the impression was allowed to form in the press that Robinson did know the dictator would be there – which she certainly didn't – and she later commented: 'It was easy to clarify and it wasn't clarified'.

The negative press coverage of Robinson's trip didn't end there. When Robinson visited a poor parish outside Santiago where Irish priests and nuns were based, *The Irish Times* headlined the visit: 'President finally makes contact with the poor of Latin America'.

There were further problems during the Brazil leg of the trip. Brazil was served by the Irish embassy in Portugal and the invites to Robinson's state dinner were sent out in European Portuguese rather than Brazilian Portuguese, prompting a nun to call RTÉ radio and outline how offensive this was. There were further reports about Robinson not visiting the poor, although the real story was that the president had been asked by a local priest not to visit the favelas in Rio because the advance police presence could cause problems for locals. 'At that stage,' Robinson later told her biographers, 'it had become the press position that I was deliberately not including these visits as part of the state visit. In other words, I was having receptions in city centre hotels to which poor priests had to travel into from the outskirts. Now normally, through the press office and through

Foreign Affairs, something like that doesn't get warped in the way it did'.

THE IMPACT

The visit certainly did spark criticism in the media of the president, who had been used to overwhelmingly positive media coverage. There was speculation that the real purpose of the South American visit and other visits was to gather support for the job of United Nations' secretary-general. *The Irish Times* editorial at the end of the trip said the tour had been 'characterised by a sequence of sour moments and rather transparent attempts at buck passing as one embarrassment succeeded another'. Posing the question as to whether Robinson was aiming to follow Boutros Boutros-Ghali as secretary general of the UN, it said that Robinson was 'suitably bashful' in her answer to a question in an interview about her interest in the top job, adding: 'Nobody would take it as a denial'.

There is no doubt that the trip marked a low point in the relationship between Robinson and both the media and the Department of Foreign Affairs. The president partly blamed Foreign Affairs for a lack of support. Her biographers concluded that 'the truth is that, for whatever reason in South America, Mary and Bride allowed the media coverage of the visit to get out of their control. They were far away and press queries were being handled by an overrun Foreign Affairs press office in Iveagh House which often couldn't even contact the president.'

Despite the problems with the trip – which the president

insisted had been very successful in terms of building trade links
– Robinson's image with the Irish public was totally
untarnished. An Independent Newspapers opinion poll carried
out a couple of weeks after her return put her popularity rating
at a staggering 92%, with 86% in favour of her staying on for
another term (which she opted not to do). There was 55%
support for Robinson's statement on the Framework
Document, although 31% felt she had overstepped the mark. A
similar figure, 32%, felt she was undertaking too many trips
abroad, although two thirds of voters were in favour of regular
trips.

Minister Jim

Charlie Haughey

THE BACKGROUND

Houdini Haughey had done it again. In November 1991 he had just fought off the fourth challenge to his leadership. After a difficult few months, when his leadership had been seriously and regularly undermined, he had defeated his former allies Albert Reynolds and Padraig Flynn and won a resounding victory, prompting the front page of *The Irish Times* to declare in its headline that 'rout of opponents puts Taoiseach in stronger position'.

THE GAFFE

A number of cabinet and junior ministerial positions had become available due to the leadership challenge. However instead of using this as an opportunity to promote loyal Junior Ministers, who had stood by him during the leadership challenge, Haughey inexplicably appointed two backbenchers Noel Davern and Jim McDaid to the cabinet.

THE IMPACT

Within a matter of hours, the decision had backfired dreadfully on Haughey, plunging his government into crisis and wiping all the benefits of his success in overcoming the leadership challenge. Many in Fianna Fáil were livid at the appointments. It was nothing against Davern or McDaid – both of whom were popular figures in the party – but there was a feeling that it was deeply unfair to those who had regularly gone out and defended the indefensible for the government. Haughey's constituency running mate Vincent Brady – who had been a loyal chief whip for a decade – was particularly angry at being overlooked once again. Junior Minister Joe Walsh was another who was disappointed. In the Dáil, the opposition criticised Davern's appointment to Education on the grounds of inexperience.

However, it was McDaid's appointment as Minister for Defence that really propelled the government into yet another major controversy and not because he had only been in the Dáil for two years at that point. A year beforehand, McDaid had been involved in an extradition case involving one of his constituents, a leading IRA man called James Pius Clarke. McDaid and Clarke had both played for St Eunan's College football team in the late 1970s. In February 1977, on the night of an attack on the home of a UDR man in County Tyrone – which resulted in the UDR man's brother-in-law being wounded – McDaid and Clarke were both attending a stag party in Letterkenny of one of their teammates.

Therefore, McDaid knew that Clarke was not involved in the attempted murder for which he had been convicted in the North. Before he became a TD he had signed a statement stating that and he, quite understandably, felt he had a moral duty to defend Clarke from being convicted of a crime that he had not committed. McDaid provided an alibi for Clarke and on 14 March, 1990, he was present at the hearing when the Supreme Court refused to extradite Clarke to the North, which the RUC had sought in relation to the shooting in Tyrone on that night in 1977. After the hearing, McDaid was photographed with Clarke on the steps of the Four Courts, in the middle of a group of anti-extradition campaigners. There was some publicity at the time and McDaid wrote to the *Irish Press,* making it clear that he supported government policy on extradition. He was also one of a number of politicians who had lobbied the Minister for Justice on the issue. Twenty months later, few in Dáil Éireann recalled the case. However, the *Belfast Telegraph* did and it ran a front-page story on McDaid's appointment to cabinet and the implications for Anglo-Irish relations.

The Workers Party and then Fine Gael picked up on the issue in the Dáil and it was also raised in the House of Commons. Fine Gael's Michael Noonan said McDaid would be perceived as a 'Provo fellow traveller' and asked Des O'Malley – the leader of the Progressive Democrats, who were Fianna Fáil's coalition partner – why he had agreed to the appointment. Noonan intimated that O'Malley should have followed the example of George Colley, the Tanaiste in Haughey's government, by insisting on a veto over who was appointed to Justice and Defence. O'Malley, who had been unaware of

McDaid's involvement in the extradition case, was immediately concerned – given the sensitive security implications involved with the Department of Defence. He expressed those concerns to Haughey. Along with PD Minister Bobby Molloy, O'Malley then met with McDaid. During that meeting the Donegal TD emphasised that he had no sympathy whatsoever with the Provisional IRA. O'Malley accepted that but felt that McDaid had compromised himself. McDaid knew that the PDs would not be able to accept his appointment and in order to head off a major confrontation between the two government parties, he went to the Taoiseach and withdrew his name. Vincent Brady became Defence Minister. In the meantime, the attack on McDaid continued in the Dáil. Fine Gael's spokesperson on Defence Madeline Taylor-Quinn provoked outrage when she said: 'I wonder now, given the proposed appointment, will the terrorist organisations of the country be privy to very secret matters?'

It was not, to put it mildly, Fine Gael's finest hour. Jim McDaid had done nothing wrong – except arguably making an error of judgment in allowing himself to be photographed outside the Four Courts with Clarke. He later pointed out that any TD would have done the same for a constituent, 'especially for someone he believed to be totally innocent'. He certainly didn't deserve the character assassination he had to endure. McDaid acted very honourably in standing aside in order to avert a crisis for his government. He got his chance to serve in cabinet six years later.

Regardless of the rights and wrongs of it, there is little doubt that Haughey made a monumental tactical error in appointing McDaid to Defence, a position that was extremely sensitive for obvious reasons. Fianna Fáil TDs were enraged by the treatment of Jim McDaid and while much of the anger was focused on the opposition, there was mutterings once again about the PD tail wagging the dog. Stephen Collins later wrote in *The Haughey File* that 'the central outcome of the affair was that Haughey having again outfoxed his internal enemies only days earlier, single handedly created a fresh political crisis. This led to renewed questioning of his judgment and put his leadership back onto the political agenda'. Bruce Arnold, in *Haughey, His Life and Unlucky Deeds* wrote that 'it was an inexplicable mistake. Carelessness had been compounded with the gratuitous insult it represented towards the party as a whole, which had been publicly shamed once more and in humiliating circumstances.' T Ryle Dwyer, in *Short Fellow – a Biography of Charles J Haughey*, wrote that following the McDaid debacle, Haughey's days as Taoiseach were numbered. And so they were. There was just 90 days to be exact from that point to his resignation from the country's most senior political job on 11 February, 1992.

Down in the Dumps
Bertie Ahern

THE BACKGROUND

Taoiseach Bertie Ahern has always been fond of presiding over openings ranging from state offices and schools to supermarkets, shops, hotels and, his critics would joke, envelopes. Ahern himself pointed out that he had opened so many places he was occasionally reduced to reopening them. Even on his holidays, it appears, Ahern was unable to resist the lure of the scissors.

In the summer of 2006, Ahern was, as usual, holidaying in South Kerry, staying with his family at the Great Southern Hotel, Parknasilla. While there, he was approached by a local businesswoman who was involved in the development of a 20 million 69-room hotel and conference centre in Sneem, the picturesque village close to Parknasilla, where Ahern regularly lunched. She asked the Taoiseach if he would visit the construction site. When he agreed, she arranged for local photographers and journalists to attend.

The following day's national newspapers ran the story of the

Taoiseach's visit to the site, with pictures of Ahern wearing a hard hat standing alongside the hotel's owner, Dublin businessman and Sneem native Louis Moriarty. In one photograph featuring Moriarty and Ahern, a tanned Taoiseach, wearing a short-sleeved shirt, was holding a 'passport' granting him access to the 'Kingdom of Kerry'. Ahern shook hands with site workmen, joking 'Up Kerry, Up the kingdom!' 'Great,' was his verdict on the project.

Moriarty said Ahern was very much part of the village and remarked that if they called a suite after him, they would attract all the Fianna Fáil supporters. It was a nice light story in the middle of the silly season . . . or so it seemed.

THE GAFFE

However, the 'great' photo opportunity quickly turned into a deep embarrassment for the Taoiseach. It emerged that Louis Moriarty had been at the centre of a series of investigations and court cases relating to some of the most serious illegal dumping ever uncovered in Ireland. Moriarty – who owned a Dublin waste disposal company, Swalcliffe Ltd, which traded as Dublin Waste – had pleaded guilty and was awaiting sentencing in relation to the charges arising out of an investigation into the biggest secret dump ever discovered in the State at the 47-acre Whitestown site in west Wicklow. He had also been the subject of a High Court Order to clean up 8,000 tonnes of waste, including hazardous clinical waste from a number of Dublin hospitals, at Coolnamadra, also in Wicklow.

THE IMPACT

Once the government became aware of Moriarty's background, it moved quickly to distance itself from the perception that Ahern had given Moriarty's new development any form of endorsement. Although Moriarty lived on Dublin's Griffith Avenue, close to Ahern's home, a spokesman stressed the Taoiseach did not know the businessman before meeting him in Sneem. 'The Taoiseach has been visiting Sneem for over 20 years,' said the spokesman. 'Last Sunday he was asked by a local person, who is known to him, to visit the development and he was glad to do it. He did so on Tuesday, the first available opportunity after the bank holiday. The visit was not in his diary. It was not an organised visit in that way. He had no prior knowledge of, or acquaintance with, Mr Louis Moriarty before the visit. The Taoiseach has absolutely nothing to say about any case pending that Mr Moriarty may be involved in,' the spokesman added.

The story was front page news the following day with the Irish *Daily Mail*'s banner-sized headline declaring: 'Bertie's holiday friend on dump charges'. The story underneath described it as 'a huge embarrassment for a man who prides himself on his political cunning'. It quoted Green Party leader Trevor Sargent saying: 'It indicates that the Taoiseach has spent a lot of money on advisers and is unable to get adequate advice'.

The embarrassment reopened the wider issue of whether it was right for the Taoiseach of the day to devote so much time to openings. Labour's deputy leader Liz McManus said: 'He will go anywhere to get a photo opportunity. He needs to take a totally new approach for the desire for publicity. He spends a lot of time promoting private operations. He needs to be a lot more circumspect about the people he associates with and be more careful about his endorsements of private individuals. It's not the job of the Taoiseach to promote private business when he should be running the country.'

The *Daily Mail's* editorial claimed that the Teflon Taoiseach was losing his touch. 'The non-stick coating that saw Mr Ahern through so many past scandals has started to wear decidedly thin. And it has to be said, the Taoiseach's legendary political instinct is also starting to look rather threadbare.' While it accepted that it was 'not exactly a resignation issue', it concluded that after almost a decade as Taoiseach 'maybe, just maybe, he should start thinking about taking a slightly longer holiday than a week in west Kerry'.

All that grief just for visiting the building site of a hotel. Ahern must have reflected on Albert Reynolds' saying about it being the little things that trip you up.

Tullymander

Jim Tully

THE BACKGROUND

Before Jack Lynch established the concept of an independent boundary commission, it was the job of the Minister for Local Government (now known as the Minister for the Environment, Heritage and Local Government) to redraw Dáil constituencies. The temptation for the incumbent Minister to shape constituencies in a manner which suited his government often proved overwhelming. In the 1960s, Fianna Fáil's Kevin Boland, as the relevant Minister, opted for three-seat constituencies in areas where Fianna Fáil was strong – with the probability that the party would win two out of three seats – and four seats in Dublin, where Fianna Fáil could potentially take two seats despite only having a minority of the vote.

Initially the revision worked well. In the 1969 general election, Fianna Fáil won 52% of the Dáil's seats with 45.7% of the vote – at the time this was a virtually unprecedented seat bonus. However, by the 1973 election, Fine Gael and Labour had agreed an electoral pact and fought the election as an alternative government. This seriously limited the benefits of the Boland constituency redrawing. While the three-seaters in rural areas had worked well for Fianna Fáil against a divided opposition, it had the opposite effect when faced with strong transfers between Fine Gael and Labour candidates. Fianna Fáil did hold its seats in Dublin, where four-seaters predominated. However, despite an increase in its overall first preference vote, the party lost six seats and power to the 'National Coalition' of Fine Gael and Labour.

It was a warning that drawing up constituencies to favour the government of the day could backfire if circumstances changed, but it was one that would be ignored by the new coalition government.

THE GAFFE

The year after the election win, new Local Government Minister Jim Tully of Labour implemented what was effectively a reverse gerrymander, which was so blatant that it will forever be remembered as the 'Tullymander'. Historian Joe Lee later wrote that it 'was the sheer professionalism of his handiwork that earned his own arrangement the half-grudging description of Tullymander, threatening to consign the venerable Governor Gerry to semantic oblivion'.

The quintessential local politician, Tully changed almost every constituency, replacing four-seater constituencies in Dublin – where Fianna Fáil was seen as weakest – with 13 three-seaters and opting for four- and five-seaters in rural areas where Fianna Fáil was strongest. It looked like a master stroke that would limit Fianna Fáil to just one out of three seats in the capital and merely an equal share of the spoils in western constituencies where it was strongest. Although some politicians, such as Garret FitzGerald, objected at cabinet to what was happening, one Fine Gael TD later wrote that 'we all rejoiced in' supporting the bill 'because we were at last getting even with Fianna Fáil, the real connoisseurs of manipulating constituency boundaries'. They were not alone. Commentators were unanimous in their lauding of Tully's plan, as Lee put it in *Ireland, 1912-1985: Politics and Society*, 'admiring his work as a masterpiece, worthy of inclusion in a hall of fame of electoral fixes'.

THE IMPACT

The problem was that the Tullymander was based on what proved to be a wildly inaccurate assumption about the likely number of votes the National Coalition would attract at the next election. Analysis carried out by Fianna Fáil's Martin O'Donoghue for his party leader in 1974 showed that if Tully's new constituencies had been in place in the 1973 general election, it would have massively benefited Fine Gael and Labour, probably increasing their majority from four to a thumping fourteen.

However, it wasn't all bad news for Fianna Fáil. O'Donoghue spotted a major weakness in Tully's proposal – it was vulnerable to any fall in the vote share of the coalition in selected constituencies. O'Donoghue later wrote that he thought Tully had made a mistake in trying to maximise the possible number of seats which Labour could win. O'Donoghue was also able to come up with an alternative redrawing of the constituencies that would minimise his party's chances of winning an overall majority, leading Fianna Fáil to the conclusion that the Tullymander was the lesser of two evils. As a result, he said, there was no systematic opposition from Fianna Fáil to the redrawing of the constituencies.

However, it was hindsight more than O'Donoghue's calculations that clearly demonstrated the huge flaw in the Tullymander – it would protect the government in the event of a minor swing against it, but a bigger swing to Fianna Fáil would bring the opposition party disproportionate gains. While a major swing against the government may have seemed improbable at the time Tully was doing his calculations, that is exactly what transpired in the 1977 landslide. Fianna Fáil won 50.6% of the vote and almost 57% of the seats – its twenty seat majority was the biggest in the history of the state. With over 50% of the vote, Fianna Fáil would have handsomely won the election regardless of the make-up of the constituencies.

Furthermore, Tully could hardly be blamed for the collapse in support for the government parties. But there is no doubt that the Tullymander inadvertently gave a hefty boost to Fianna Fáil's majority. Instead of winning one out of three seats as planned, the size of Fianna Fáil's vote meant the party took two out of three seats in many constituencies. In four seaters, it was also in with a chance of taking three of the seats. The result was a disaster for Labour, with two ministers – Justin Keating and Conor Cruise O'Brien – losing their seats. This left the party with no obvious successor to Brendan Corish who, along with outgoing Taoiseach Liam Cosgrave, announced his resignation as party leader immediately after the election.

Despite overseeing a massive increase in public housing during his ministry, Tully was not going to be a potential candidate given the Tullymander disaster. 'Tully suddenly found himself in near disgrace after his apparently foolproof constituency revision had so unsportingly backfired,' Joe Lee wrote. He did, however, go on to become deputy leader of the party under Michael O'Leary in 1981 and he was Minister for Defence in the shortlived 1981/82 Fine Gael-Labour coalition. While fulfilling those duties, he was present at the military parade in Cairo when Egyptian President Anwar Sadat was assassinated. Tully suffered a shrapnel injury to the face and retired from politics in 1982. There is no doubt but that some good did come out of the Tullymander. Jack Lynch, to his credit, delivered on a pre-election promise contained on page one of Fianna Fáil's general election manifesto to establish an independent boundary review commission, thereby ending forever the highly undesirable practice of the Minister of the day dictating the make-up of the Dáil constituencies.

The Hand of History

Tony Blair

THE BACKGROUND

It was April 1998 and the quest for peace in Northern Ireland – after almost three decades of the Troubles – was close to a major breakthrough. After months of negotiations involving all political parties, a deadline of Easter weekend was set by Chairman of the talks, US senator George Mitchell. 'These guys had talked for nearly two years – they could talk for 20 years if given the opportunity. It was at that point I concluded that the only possibility for success required an early, fixed and unbreakable deadline, which I thought after looking at the calendar, should be Easter Weekend,' Mitchell later recalled.

THE GAFFE

An understandably excited Tony Blair – who had been British Prime Minister for less than a year at that point but had already made an enormous impact with his fresh approach to the North

THE TROUBLES

I feel the hand of history on our shoulders!

– arrived in Belfast on the Tuesday prior to the endgame negotiations. He told waiting reporters that 'a day like today is not a day for sound bites, really we can leave them at home. But I feel the hand of history upon our shoulders, in respect of this, I really do. I just think we need to acknowledge that and respond to it. Now maybe it's impossible to find a way through. Maybe even with the best faith in the world, we can't do it. But it's right to try and I'm here to try.'

THE IMPACT

The remark unintentionally brought a moment of levity to the almost crushing tension of the occasion. Although everybody understood what Blair meant – the hand of history was indeed on their shoulders – his stated warning about it not being a day for sound bites meant there was much chuckling when he said it. However, Blair, cringy or not, helped to deliver the result.

Three days later on Good Friday 1998, Mitchell was able to tell the media: 'I'm pleased to announce that the two governments and the political parties of Northern Ireland have reached agreement. The Agreement proposes changes in the Irish Constitution and in British constitutional law to enshrine the principle that it is the people of Northern Ireland who will decide, democratically, their own future'. Blair himself commented: 'I said when I arrived here that I felt the hand of history upon us. Today I hope that the burden of history can at long last start to be lifted from our shoulders.'

It was a hugely historic moment. While many difficult days would lie ahead for the peace process, the Good Friday

Agreement was endorsed in referenda north and south of the border and it was clear to most people that a point of no-return had been passed. However, the fact that history was made didn't stop more than 45,000 people from voting Blair's remarks as the most embarrassing political moment of all time in a poll on the BBC's *The Politics Show* some years later. Perhaps a tad unfair, given that no UK Prime Minister has done more to help bring about peace in Northern Ireland. But that's politics for you.

The Blood Scandal

Michael Noonan

THE BACKGROUND

In February 1994, the Irish Blood Transfusion Board (BTSB) admitted that some women may have been infected with the Hepatitis C virus from contaminated Anti-D, a product some-times given to women in childbirth. While it took years for the full story to emerge, over 1,000 women were found to be infected with the virus. The shocking news caused a massive political controversy, led to the creation of two tribunals of inquiry and prompted the broadcasting of a powerful docu-drama which was screened on RTÉ in early 2002. The State had to pay over €600 million in compensation to the women affected. Legal fees alone accounted for €70 million.

An impressive campaign group, Positive Action, was set up to fight for those infected, led by journalist Jane O'Brien. O'Brien later won the Person of the Year Award. The first woman to die from the contaminated blood was Brigid McCole, a mother of 12 from Donegal, who to this day remains a household name in Ireland. She died in October 1996 after a marathon legal battle with the State for compensation. The BTSB, despite its own negligence, had threatened her with the prospect of facing enormous legal costs if she pursued her claim for compensation in the High Court.

After her death, public outrage at the manner in which the government had fought a legal case against a very ill woman effectively left the Health Minister, Michael Noonan, with no option but to set up a judicial inquiry. Just weeks earlier, he had refused to contemplate this. Now, with extremely broad terms of reference, the inquiry would also examine the role of the Department of Health in the events that had taken place. Noonan was not in any way responsible for the infection of the women – the events took place long before he became Health Minister. However, he had the political misfortune to be in charge of the Department of Health as the scandal unfolded. He came under serious pressure regarding the State's handling of compensation claims by the victims and what was perceived to be a clinical, legalistic response by the government.

To succeed in the compensation tribunal, the victims had to drop any claim against the Department of Health, something the opposition claimed was akin to a cover-up. Speaking in the Dáil in October 1996, in the wake of the decision to set up the judicial inquiry, Noonan declared that what had happened was 'nothing less than a public health disaster' and he described the events of recent years as 'a scandal'. It was a careful exercise, *The Irish Times* reported the following day, 'designed to ring fence his Department against attack. And then he blew it'.

THE GAFFE

An angry and hurt Noonan went on to defend his decision to set up the original compensation tribunal for the Hepatitis C victims, arguing that the courts were unsuitable as a vehicle for awarding compensation in 'cases arising from tragic events with a large number of plaintiffs who have broadly similar claims'. The compensation tribunal offered victims an 'unprecedented forum where their claims are, in effect, unopposed'. Compensation could be obtained 'without any opposition, with no risk of cross-examination'. He added: 'It is not surprising that none of the 140 awards has been rejected. I ask the House to contrast this with the court system which is adversarial with all which that implies'.

However, the real problem arose when Noonan posed the question as to whether 'on reflection, would not the solicitors for the plaintiff have served their client better if they had advised her to go to the compensation tribunal early this year? Is it not accepted in the legal profession that the tribunal is working well and that Mrs. McCole could have received a significantly higher award by going before it? She would not have had to face the enormous stress of court proceedings. Could her solicitors not, in selecting a test case from the hundreds of hepatitis C cases on their books, have selected a plaintiff in a better condition to sustain the stress of a High Court case? Was it in the interest of their client to attempt to run her case not only in the High Court, but also in the media and the Dáil simultaneously?'

THE IMPACT

Immediate, enormous and long-lasting. The attack had been aimed at the lawyers, but the Positive Action group, watching in the public gallery of the Dáil, saw it as an attack on a dead woman and on themselves for challenging the State in the courts. They walked out of the gallery and immediately demanded that Noonan should apologise or resign.

Noonan was in serious trouble and politically isolated. 'Within an hour', *The Irish Times* reported, 'the Minister was dressed in sackcloth and ashes and was rending his clothes on the floor of the Dáil.' He told the house that he now realised his comments on the late Mrs McCole's legal proceedings have 'caused understandable offence to her family, to other victims and to those in the organisation associated with the campaign and I would like to avail of this opportunity to apologise unreservedly for any offence. It was not intended in any way whatsoever. I certainly did not mean to question in any way the right of Mrs McCole and her legal team to take the course of action which they did. It is a great personal tragedy for the family and Mrs McCole and I apologise again for any hurt I may have caused. I was making criticisms of the adversarial legal system and in the course of an adversarial legal system sometimes contending parties can cause difficulty. I made the remarks in that context. There was no intention of hurting or offending Mrs. McCole's family in any way whatsoever.'

While the apology was heartfelt and genuine, the damage was done. Any goodwill generated by the government as a result of establishing the tribunal of inquiry was swept away by those few angry words.

Noonan, previously regarded as the safest pair of hands in Fine Gael, never fully recovered from his handling of this issue. A formidable and extremely competent politician, Noonan went on to become leader of Fine Gael in 2001, successfully challenging John Bruton and overcoming Enda Kenny in the subsequent leadership contest, but his tenure in the job was disastrous. Just before becoming leader, Noonan sought to address the Hepatitis C issue head on, admitting he had handled it badly. He told RTÉ: 'If I was doing it again I would not do it the way I did it. I relied on legal advice, and I should have relied more on political advice.' Noonan said he accepted the criticisms made of him that he should have intervened with the BTSB to prevent them from taking such an aggressive legal stance with Brigid McCole.

Over a year later, at the party's Ard Fheis in 2002, just months before the general election, Noonan again sought to bring an end to the controversy, declaring he had 'made a mistake in the handling of the case of the late Mrs Brigid McCole', adding: 'as I have said on more than one occasion, I deeply regret that I handled it the way I did and I again sincerely apologise to the McCole family for the grief caused to them. This has been one of the most significant experiences in my personal and political life and I want to assure you that any government I may lead will not make a similar mistake in the future.'

But his comments failed to bring the desired political closure and the issue haunted him throughout his leadership. His credibility was seriously undermined with the public constantly reminded of the Brigid McCole case by the media and Fine Gael's political rivals. The screening of the *No Tears* docu-drama on RTÉ – featuring a character described as 'the Minister' which was clearly based on Noonan – certainly did not help in the run-up to the 2002 election. Noonan described the series as 'unfair' and 'legally very risky' and received public support from one Hepatitis C victim who said he had been turned into a 'stage villain'. But the on-going fallout was certainly a factor in his poor personal ratings throughout his leadership. Fine Gael received a drubbing in the 2002 General Election, losing 23 seats and Noonan immediately resigned as leader. The man supposed to be part of a 'dream team' leadership with Jim Mitchell simply never recovered from his nightmare spell in the Department of Health.

Harsh Medicine

Bertie Ahern

THE BACKGROUND

It was December 2004 and the Fianna Fáil/Progressive Democrats government was having more than its share of difficulties. The 'f**king peace process', to paraphrase John Bruton (see Chapter 2), was proving as infuriating as ever. An historic deal on the North – which promised to bring total IRA decommissioning of arms and a power-sharing Northern Executive and Assembly – had failed to materialise at the last minute, largely due to the issue of photographic verification of IRA decommissioning. Republicans balked at the photographs, claiming they were designed to humiliate, not to verify. They also cited comments made by DUP leader Ian Paisley about 'humiliating' republicans as one of the reasons for the failure to fully resolve the decommissioning issue. The DUP, in turn, blamed Sinn Féin for the failure to conclude a deal. It all seemed depressingly familiar. But the Taoiseach's problems hadn't started – or finished – with the collapse of the deal.

A week before the talks collapsed, Ahern landed himself in

trouble when he was asked by Fine Gael leader Enda Kenny about the state of the talks on the North and whether the release of the killers of Garda Jerry McCabe was on the agenda. Instead of fudging the question, Ahern was uncharacteristically forthcoming in his response. 'To be frank and open . . . this is the place to say it . . . it is my belief that if we are to have a comprehensive agreement, this is an issue that will have to be part of the final deal.' Kenny, sensing potential difficulty for the government, asked Ahern to elaborate. 'Am I to understand the Taoiseach is confirming that, in the context of a successful conclusion to the discussions which are at a sensitive stage, the killers of the late Detective Garda McCabe will be given early release?'

The Taoiseach replied that obviously the government would have to consult the McCabe family and the gardaí, but added: 'This is not a question on which I want to have ambiguity. If we are to have a comprehensive deal, this matter will be part of it and I would recommend that that be the case. I do not see how we will be able to deal with it otherwise.'

The comments came on the morning of the budget, which tempered the reaction temporarily. A major political storm sprang up which negated the positive news in Brian Cowen's first budget. After enduring a difficult couple of years since its re-election, that was the last thing the government needed. Government TDs were puzzled as to why the Taoiseach had been so forthright, especially when there was no guarantee of a deal on the North the following week. The belief was that Ahern thought it would be a good idea to get the issue out of the way on budget day, in the belief that it would be overtaken by budget news.

If that was the case, the Taoiseach was seriously mistaken.

With the deal on the North collapsing, Ahern had the worst of both worlds – he had publicly made politically damaging concessions, but then couldn't deliver an agreement. However, if the Taoiseach thought things couldn't get any worse, he was about to find out how wrong he was.

THE GAFFE

Ahern met with Sinn Féin's Gerry Adams and Martin McGuinness at his constituency headquarters in Drumcondra. Emerging from the meeting, he told the media that the issue of photographs was 'not workable, so we have to try and find some other way'. Standing alongside the Taoiseach, Adams chipped in that 'the photograph was never a runner, particularly since Ian Paisley described it as being part of a process of humiliation'. Ahern's comments were clearly seen as supporting the Sinn Féin position on photographs just five days after his government had accepted the need for photographs at a joint press conference in Belfast with the British Prime Minister Tony Blair. The Taoiseach's words were guaranteed to enrage the DUP.

THE IMPACT

Suitably enraged, the DUP immediately broke off contact with the government, demanding an apology. 'From day one until now Mr Ahern never opposed photographs, and [he] suddenly meets two IRA/Sinn Féiners and comes out and says: "It's not workable, that's out". So anything the IRA says is not workable, he will bow to. He double-crossed Mrs McCabe, he'll not double-cross us,' Ian Paisley acidly observed.

Since becoming Taoiseach in 1997, Ahern had handled the Northern peace process with remarkable skill and diplomacy. Now his comments had provoked the DUP into saying it would not deal with Foreign Affairs Minister Dermot Ahern or government officials at planned talks involving the Northern Secretary and other parties at Hillsborough Castle the following day.

Bertie Ahern had made a major boo-boo and now he would have to swallow some particularly unpalatable medicine to make amends. Four decades earlier, Paisley had thrown snowballs at the car of Fianna Fáil Taoiseach Sean Lemass when he visited Belfast and now this Fianna Fáil Taoiseach was going to have to beg forgiveness from the DUP leader. It couldn't have been easy for him but Ahern, putting the peace process before his pride, issued a full apology to Paisley in a nine-minute phone call, during which he emphasised that the government still wanted IRA decommissioning to be photographed.

'The Taoiseach apologised for any confusion that this might have caused, and reassured Reverend Paisley that the Irish Government had not abandoned the proposals of last week,' a government spokeswoman said.

Keen to bring an end to the controversy as quickly as possible, government sources didn't try and hide the fact that Ahern had blundered. 'Ian Paisley was very, very upset,' one source was quoted in the media as saying. 'I think some people were a little worried that the reverend wouldn't take the call.'

Ahern's apology may have been difficult but it had the desired effect. A spokesman for the DUP said Ahern had met the party's primary requirements during his phone call. He told *The Irish Times* that once the Taoiseach made his position clear publicly – probably in his statement during the Dáil debate on the British-Irish 'Comprehensive Agreement' the following day – 'then DUP members would be free to have talks with Dermot Ahern at Hillsborough later'.

Paisley himself told the same newspaper: 'I asked for an apology, a full apology. I told him that if he wanted to change his mind, he was entitled to do that, but he is entitled to ring me first and say "I am changing my mind and backing out of this agreement, I don't agree with the photographs". But he [Ahern] said: "I do agree with the photographs".' Paisley added: 'Then I read to him what he said, and he [Ahern] said: "Yes, that was very badly put, I admit that".' The DUP leader then asked the Taoiseach if he was now making the apology which was sought, to which Ahern replied. 'Yes, I give you a full apology, and I regret that you were offended.'

A Fianna Fáil Taoiseach ringing Ian Paisley to apologise to him – changed times indeed.

That Twink-ing Feeling
John Bruton / Eoghan Harris

THE BACKGROUND

May 1991 and Fine Gael was enduring some difficult times. The party was struggling to cope in the post-FitzGerald era. It dumped Alan Dukes, the successor to Garret FitzGerald, in the previous year after a disastrous performance in the presidential election. However, a change of leadership didn't bring any dramatic improvement in the fortunes of what was a deeply divided party.

New leader John Bruton brought in Eoghan Harris as media advisor. Intelligent and articulate, mercurial and with a long and varied CV – which includes success as a screenwriter for the critically acclaimed Carlton TV drama series *Sharpe* – the one-time RTÉ producer was best known in political circles for his influential involvement in Mary Robinson's successful presidential election campaign the previous year. Fine Gael made a decision to abandon the normal Ard Fheis in that year. There was a view, not just in Fine Gael, that the traditional Ard Fheis format had become dated. Instead the party opted for a

special one-day convention with the theme of unemployment – then the number one issue in politics. The conference's slogan was 'Fast Forward with Fine Gael'. By the time the conference was over, it seemed the party was going to be permanently stuck in reverse.

THE GAFFE

As a warm-up to the day's proceedings, the fatal decision was made to present a comedy sketch, featuring well-known comedienne Twink. The ten-minute sketch, written mainly by Harris and broadcast live on television, included a string of, what *The Irish Times* the following Monday described as, 'unsavoury jokes'.

Twink, playing the part of Bernie, a cleaning lady of Jumbo toilet rolls advertisement fame, began by saying John Bruton had given her a tip for a job in the Dáil – he had told her to follow Pee Flynn and Ned O'Keeffe around and clean up after them. 'Send the bill around to Charlie. You'll never be out of work again, sez John.'

It wasn't long before delegates had become 'visibly uncomfortable' at the content which included references to French kissing, the PDs 'in bed with Charlie' and a TD who had come at her with something 18 inches long – 'you have a filty dirty mind. It was his tongue I was talking about', she quipped to an audience member.

THE IMPACT

Fine Gael certainly hit the headlines with its special one-day conference, but for all the wrong reasons. While some of the reaction may have been a bit po-faced, the sketch quite plainly did not work. The next day's *Sunday Press* splashed with the story, headlined: 'Naughty Twink sinks FG's Harris-Fheis'. The story opened: 'Fine Gael's new style 'mini Ard Fheis' was totally overshadowed by Twink's opening contribution on live TV which deeply offended many delegates and TDs with a series of blue jokes.' The report said that most delegates found the jokes 'smutty and offensive in the extreme', adding that a smaller number walked out in protest.

Senior figures in Fine Gael did not disagree. Ivan Yates apologised for any offence caused, while delegates and parliamentary party members generally 'expressed dismay at its lewdness'. John Bruton exacerbated the damage by refusing to apologise for the sketch, although he stressed that no hurt was intended. 'If you have a comedian and you start applying very rigorous criteria to comedy as you do to politics, all comedy would be the subject of an apology,' he said.

In theory, Bruton was right, politically he was completely wrong. The Fine Gael leader also defended the lack of vetting of the script. 'You cannot get into a situation where you have filtered comedy. I did not see the script. I did not ask to see the script. We did not tell Twink what to say. It's perfectly plain. It was comedy,' he said.

Whether it was comedy or not was a matter of opinion but it certainly didn't mix well with politics. There was a queue of people to condemn the sketch. Fianna Fáil sources described it as 'ghastly and in appalling bad taste'. While tut-tutting from the old enemy might be expected, traditional coalition partner Labour did not pull its punches. A spokesman said Bruton's 'refusal to disassociate himself did him no credit at all. When the victim becomes the butt of televised humour, it demeans the people putting it in. It was cheap, sordid and dishonourable.'

Liz O'Donnell, vice chairwoman of the Women's Political Association at the time, said it was in disbelief and sadness she listened to Bruton's refusal, on RTÉ Radio One's flagship show *This Week*, to apologise for the 'blatantly sexist and hugely offensive comedy sketch'.

Twink, meanwhile, told journalists that while the script was written by Harris, she would like to think she 'added the touches and timing'. For about 90% of the sketch, she had adhered to what Harris – whom she described as 'a political genius' – had written. She thought it was excellent satire and it was time in Ireland that we woke up to good political haranguing. The comedienne stressed she did not mean to offend and that the sketch was intended to get a laugh.

True to form, Harris was – and remains to this day – totally unrepentant, arguing it was fair comment. 'If Fianna Fáil gives a target of opportunity like Ned O'Keefe, and before that Padraig Flynn, we are going to hit it'.

Although most people in Fine Gael agreed the party had only succeeded in hitting itself in the foot, Harris argued that 'only toffee-nosed people would be annoyed'. Harris said he was puzzled by critical comments made by the party's MEP Mary Banotti, since she seemed to be enjoying the sketch at the time. Banotti issued a statement saying she regretted Harris' statement and she took 'grave exception' to references to a political dimension to her objections to those events. The political dimension to her objections, referred to by Harris, was presumably her support for former leader Alan Dukes.

An editorial on the following Monday in *The Irish Times* headlined 'High ideals, cheap laughs', was critical of the 'inexcusable' decision to use content based on 'an incident painful to private citizens to raise a cheap laugh'. It added: 'Fine Gael's planners and Mr Bruton, who accused Fianna Fáil of displaying a feudal attitude to women, must bear the responsibility'. The editorial concluded that the leader's suggestion that he had nothing to apologise for would be regarded by colleagues – who showed more sensitivity – as 'compounding an error which reflected poor judgment in the first place'.

The debacle had a hugely demoralising impact on Fine Gael and there is no doubt that it seriously damaged the party's credibility with the electorate. Bruton and his party continued to struggle in the opinion polls and had a disastrous general election performance the following year, losing ten seats, although clearly this could not be entirely blamed on the embarrassment of 18 months earlier. In the wake of that election, the party had to suffer the humiliation of its traditional coalition partner, Labour, choosing to go into government with Fianna Fáil.

While the Twink sketch will be remembered for many years to come, the impact on Bruton's political fortunes was not long term. In late 1994, the Fianna Fáil/Labour government collapsed and Bruton achieved his destiny, becoming Taoiseach for two-and-a-half years. It is generally recognised that he excelled in the position and, but for a poor decision by the Rainbow government about the timing of the 1997 general election, he might have been in the job for a decade.

Gerry Meandering

Gerry Collins

THE BACKGROUND

In November 1991, the rumblings of discontent throughout the preceding months concerning the leadership of Charlie Haughey finally came to a head. Following a heated parliamentary party meeting, backbencher Sean Power, one of the 'Gang of Four' TDs who had criticised the Taoiseach in late September, put down a formal motion calling for Haughey's removal as party leader. Albert Reynolds, who just weeks earlier had backed off a potential challenge, announced his support for the motion. A heavyweight confrontation was looming: the Minister of Finance was taking on the Taoiseach of the day and there could be only one winner. There turned out, however, to be more than one loser.

THE GAFFE

Foreign Affairs Minister Gerry Collins went into RTÉ's Dáil studio to do an interview for the evening news, immediately prior to an interview with Albert Reynolds. A legendary political operator, the usually unflappable Collins gave a hugely emotional performance, where he appeared close to tears at times. During the bizzare interview, he pleaded – and *pleaded* is very definitely the word – with Reynolds not to 'wreck our party'. He said that although Reynolds 'means well', what he was doing was 'so wrong'. Reynolds should draw back and face up to his responsibilities. This was a time for 'extreme political maturity'. The government had its problems, but it was successful and Reynolds' declaration that he was going 'to try and vote Charles Haughey out of office and take it on for himself' would 'wreck our party right down the centre. It's going to bust up the government and it's certainly not going to serve the best interests of the people.'

While one commentator later wrote that the 'condemnatory tone of Mr Collins was striking', Collins insisted during the interview that he would not condemn Reynolds. 'Albert Reynolds and I would not condemn each other for anything. We have worked together for a considerable period of time, but I totally disagree with his tactics. I think it shows a frightful political immaturity.' Reynolds had 'boxed' himself in, 'unwisely and unnecessarily so', a couple of weeks earlier when he said on radio he would have won a no-confidence resolution had it been placed at that time.

Asked by interviewer Sean Duignan if it was not best to clear the air about the leadership, Collins responded: 'If Albert

Reynolds were talking about, and I'm sure he means well, trying to do away with instability, surely he can see that what he is doing is going to create far greater instability and leads us into a chaotic situation in a matter of 24 or 48 hours. I believe that what Albert is doing now is so wrong that he should pull back from wrecking the government and throwing the country into panic and chaos and I, for my part, am supporting the Taoiseach. I trust him. I respect his authority, his office and the dignity of his office.'

And, before a huge television audience, he concluded with a direct appeal to Reynolds: 'And I might say, Albert, before you vote and before you issue this particular statement in the form it is, Albert, face up to your responsibilities and if you feel as solemnly as you believe you do, well then, you've no option but to give us your resignation . . . before you vote on Saturday'.

THE IMPACT

The impact on Albert Reyolds? Zilch, but it was a different story for the nation as a whole and on Collins himself. The following weekend in *The Irish Times*, Dick Walsh summed it up neatly when he said that Collins hadn't been addressing Sean Duignan and he 'may not even have been talking to the audience, which by now was rolling in the aisles, perhaps in panic and chaos, certainly in convulsions'. Gerry – Walsh noted caustically that 'we are on first name terms here' – had his eye on Albert. 'And as he was led away, weeping into a big white handkerchief that he'd bought somewhere foreign, he was replaced on screen by Albert, who seemed remarkably unmoved by the outburst.'

On the same day, Drapier – the anonymous columnist in *The Irish Times* advised Haughey to 'keep Collins off the airwaves for the duration. The latter's performance on Thursday's RTÉ news will be remembered for a long time. Haughey can do without such support.'

Writing in *Short Fellow – a Biography of Charles J Haughey*, T. Ryle Dwyer described Collins' 'tear jerking appeal' as a 'ridiculous performance' and said 'Collins effectively destroyed whatever chance he had of succeeding Haughey himself'. Up to that point Collins had been regarded as a 'dark horse' in the succession stakes.

Dwyer noted that this was the first political crisis where TV cameras had been in the Dáil. There had been some unruly scenes in the Dáil and, he said, 'the whole thing was beginning to look like a bad political play in which ham actors were turning tragedy into a farce'. Collins' interview would later be famously parodied by Dermot Morgan and would live longer in the memory than the actual leadership challenge.

Within a couple of hours of Collins' outburst, Haughey fired Reynolds from the cabinet, with Padraig Flynn – a strong Reynolds supporter – following suit soon after. A couple of days later Haughey survived the leadership challenge, comfortably winning a vote in the parliamentary party by 55 votes to 22. However, his victory was short-lived and within four months he was succeeded by Reynolds. Not surprisingly, Collins was one of the victims of Reynolds' purge of the old cabinet when he took over. Collins never served in cabinet again. However, he became an MEP in 1994 until he lost his seat a decade later. He retired from politics at that point after almost four decades – 13 of which were as a cabinet minister – on the national scene.

Jobs for the Boys

Oliver J Flanagan

THE BACKGROUND

Few politicians in the history of the Irish State are as well remembered today as Oliver J Flanagan – quite an achievement given that he served only briefly as a cabinet minister as well as having two spells as a Junior Minister. During his 43 years as a TD for Laois-Offaly – first as an Independent TD and then with Fine Gael – he was rarely shy about voicing his opinions.

An ultra-conservative Catholic, he was once described as the most right-wing politician in Ireland. His best remembered line, uttered on the *Late Late Show* that 'sex never came to Ireland until Telifis Éireann went on the air' is almost always interpreted far too literally. Flanagan was joking and four decades on, it is still a particularly astute observation.

It's harder to put a positive spin on his anti-Semitic Dáil speech of July 1943, while four years later the Locke Tribunal Report was damning in its assessment of his claims against members of the Fianna Fáil government in relation to the

Locke's Distillery scandal. The Report found that the charge of involvement of a Fianna Fáil politician in the scandal was 'wholly untrue' and 'entirely without foundation', and that it was made with 'a degree of recklessness amounting to complete irresponsibility'. The judges also said that during the tribunal Flanagan was 'very uncandid and much disposed to answer unthinkingly and as if he were directing his replies elsewhere than to the tribunal' (the approach seemed to work – in the following year's general election his vote increased by almost half to over 14,000).

'Uncandid' was not a word that would ordinarily be associated with Flanagan. During an appearance on the *Late Late Show* in February 1968, the outspoken TD's candidness got him into a fair amount of hot water. There was a referendum pending which proposed changing Ireland's electoral system from Proportional Representation (Single Transferable Vote) to a first-past-the-post system. Fine Gael was opposed to any change. On the *Late Late Show*, Flanagan admitted that he was personally in favour of such a change but that he would be doing his party's bidding and working for the preservation of PR. He explained that he was a 'loyal party member' and he would 'do what the leader of my party wishes me to do'. While he expressed his own personal views, as a member of a political party he had to accept the majority view and 'fall into line'.

It was a refreshingly honest statement and one many observers would have regarded as admirable. However, for some of his party, Flanagan was about to become a little too honest.

THE GAFFE

The programme's subject for discussion changed to political influence with regard to jobs. That weekend's *Sunday Press* reported on its front page that 'Mr Flanagan with a slight grin caused raised eyebrows when he said he firmly believed in "jobbery".' Flanagan said that although 'my party does not believe in jobbery, I am a firm and convinced believer in it. I do not see anything wrong in a TD getting a job for a friend. I have found jobs over the past 25 years for numerous people from Laois-Offaly and Dublin and any time I hear of Fianna Fáil ministers being criticised for putting their friends into jobs, I am angered because I am not in the same position to put my friends in jobs.'

THE IMPACT

Flanagan may simply have been voicing what many TDs privately believed but his views did not go down well with members of his own party. A few nights later, Garret FitzGerald, then a senator, was speaking in a debate at Trinity College Historical Society on the motion that 'Fianna Fáil has betrayed the Republic'. After what the *Irish Press* described as a 'long harangue against the ineffectiveness of Fianna Fáil', FitzGerald 'turned vitriolic TV critic' of Oliver J's weekend *Late Late* performance. 'People who believe in jobbery have no place in Fine Gael. Such people are not fit to hold office in a Fine Gael government,' said the future Taoiseach in what the newspaper described as an 'unexpected washing of one's own linen'. Flanagan's comments were, FitzGerald said, in direct conflict with Fine Gael's stated policy, published at the time of the recent local elections, that there should be an end to the system of political appointments.

Flanagan's response came in the form of a statement. Dr FitzGerald, he said 'is an economist and I am a politician and economists do not make good politicians. Free discussion is the essence of democracy and there is nothing wrong with discussing freely, without committing one's political party, the present system of appointments. Senator FitzGerald may have another system. The US has another which I personally favour.' Flanagan said that he had made it clear in the discussion that he was putting forward his own personal ideas. 'Are we in public life to go around with muzzles on our mouths? The real essence of democracy is that one should speak one's mind. I am prepared to defend the right of expressing free personal views provided I make it clear I am not committing my party to them.'

Not surprisingly, Flanagan added that he had no intention of quitting Fine Gael, stating: 'I have the greatest affection, loyalty and admiration for Mr [Liam] Cosgrave [Fine Gael leader]. My regard for him is too great that I should consider for one moment the invitation of the senator.' He pointedly concluded: 'I excuse Senator FitzGerald because he is new to public life. When he is 25 years in the Dáil he will be much wiser in the matter of getting votes.'

Writing in his autobiography – almost 25 years later – FitzGerald recalled his 'public disagreement' with Flanagan 'on the issue of jobbery, which I strongly opposed'. He said that two Fine Gael councillors had 'taken exception' to Flanagan's 'support for "jobs for the boys" ' and criticised Cosgrave for nominating Flanagan to replace him at the consecration of a bishop. At a subsequent party meeting, FitzGerald listed the differences between Fianna Fáil and Fine Gael, including 'our parties' divergent attitudes' to jobbery and corruption. However, according to FitzGerald, Cosgrave chose to attack the two councillors, whose comments had not featured in the debate, and referred approvingly to Flanagan's senior position in the party. 'This was seen as a disguised attack on me,' FitzGerald wrote. It would not be the last time that tension surfaced between the liberal/social democratic and Christian democratic wings of Fine Gael.

Although the two men were on opposing wings of the party, FitzGerald and Flanagan later served in the same cabinet. Flanagan became Minister for Defence, succeeding Paddy Donegan after the latter's 'thundering disgrace' remarks (see Chapter 43) in 1976. FitzGerald went on to become very 'wise in the matter of getting votes'. As party leader, he brought Fine Gael to within five seats of Fianna Fáil. Not surprisingly, Flanagan did not serve as a minister under FitzGerald.

In 1986, in keeping with his belief that politicians 'should speak one's mind', he campaigned against the divorce referendum even though the Fine Gael-led government proposed it. Although there was much tut-tutting at Flanagan's remarks about jobbery, no government in the ensuing four decades did anything to end the system of 'jobs for the boys'.

Chemical Cuffe

Ciaran Cuffe

THE BACKGROUND

The Green Party had its most successful election ever in Ireland in 2002, resulting in the election of six deputies to the Dáil. Among the four new deputies was the representative for Dún Laoghaire Ciaran Cuffe, who became the party's Environment and Justice spokesman.

THE GAFFE

Cuffe had inherited a €1m-plus portfolio of shares from his mother but it emerged in the TD's register of interests that the portfolio included shares in 'politically incorrect' ventures. They included a firm fined for pollution in Angola, one excluded from the Catholic Church's investment list due to arms links and chemical dumping and a company found guilty of contaminating water in Ireland.

THE IMPACT

The story was deeply embarrassing both for Cuffe and the Greens, with the party's political opponents glorying in their discomfort. Cuffe stood down as the party's Environment spokesman – although continuing in the Justice position – admitting he was naïve to hold shares linked to chemical dumping and arms. While he noted that he had not chosen the shares, inheriting them from his mother who had passed away three years earlier, he said he had been uncomfortable with his portfolio and had intended doing something about it and regretted not doing so. 'I should have paid attention to this sooner. It has been a busy year for me. I was elected a year ago. With my second son being born eight months ago, it had been on my mind but it has been busy,' he said.

His party leader Trevor Sargent said there was no case for Cuffe resigning from the party. 'Had Ciaran gone out and bought these shares and tried to keep them secret, it would have been a resigning matter. But this is somebody who lost their mother. There is a human side to this story. This was an oversight and he is having to pay the price for it.' Cuffe promised to get rid of the shares 'within a matter of months, if not weeks'. He duly did so, re-investing in ethical funds, including shares in Condomi, a German company which manufactures condoms.

A Double Whammy
Progressive Democrats

THE BACKGROUND

1997 was a general election year and the Progressive Democrats entered it in fine fettle. The first national opinion poll of 1997, carried out by IMS in the *Irish Independent*, showed the PDs at 11% nationwide and 16% in Dublin. A subsequent MRBI poll in *The Irish Times* put the party at 9%. The PDs looked well placed to build on its 1992 general election result – when the party won ten seats – and enter government with Fianna Fáil at the expense of the Rainbow coalition.

THE GAFFE

When the party's election manifesto, 'A New Deal', was rolled out on 21 May, it contained two proposals that would almost sink the PDs. The first, under the heading 'Supporting the Family', promised to 'bring in measures to encourage young single mothers to remain with their families rather than set up one-parent homes'. The second undertook to cut the numbers employed in the public service by 25,000 over five years.

THE IMPACT

Both proposals went down like lead balloons. Initially, it was the measure on young single mothers that attracted the most controversy. The proposal was actually quite moderate and could have been perceived as the beginning of a welcome debate about how best the State could assist single parents. At the press conference to launch the manifesto, Harney said that 'an incentive should be given to a young single mother to remain with her family and some of that money should be used to provide back-up parenting assistance that a young mother in that situation requires'.

However, as pointed out by Stephen Collins in his book *Breaking the Mould – How the PDs Changed Irish Politics*, while the party was 'attempting to be at the cutting edge of social policy to prove their distinctiveness', it had 'inadvertently handed a loaded gun to its enemies at a critical time in the campaign'. Collins recalls that 'Harney began to realise this during the press conference when she had to defend herself against a few well-known journalists who accused her of 'going back to the bad old days' and 'stigmatising illegitimacy'.

Harney protested that she did not propose to cut any benefits. 'What is more compassionate: a system that forces young single mothers to isolate themselves in council houses away from human contact and support in order to receive benefits, or one

which provides them with the option to live with the father of the child or with their own family?'

Although in hindsight the logic of Harney's argument is hard to fault – in fact a Labour TD had made similar comments in an earlier newspaper article – the PDs were onto a massive loser. As Harney later admitted, a general election campaign was not the time to raise such a serious issue. One national newspaper's editorial said there was 'something odious' in what 'is essentially a proposal for behaviour modification'. The measure reflected a 'dubious order of priorities while so many aspects of these young girls' lives are fundamentally disadvantaged and when the conditions in which they exist are often cruel and deprived,' it said.

However, while more of a slow burner, it was probably the proposal to cut 25,000 public service jobs that ultimately proved most damaging to the PDs. It was politically crazy to go into a general election campaign promising to cut so many jobs. Not surprisingly, the public sector unions and employees reacted with outright hostility to the idea.

To this day, there is confusion in the ranks of the PDs as to who was responsible for the two controversial policies. Mary Harney has said the figure of 25,000 mentioned in the proposal was the result of a genuine mathematical error. 'It was supposed to be 1% of something but it came out as 10%,' she said. But whoever was responsible, as Stephen Collins wrote, instead of generating a debate as Harney had hoped, these two proposals enabled left-wing parties and much of the media to portray the PDs as launching an unsympathetic attack on the most vulnerable in society – keen to rein in single mothers and sack thousands of public servants.

The campaign proved a disaster for the PDs. The party was

riven by recriminations and in-fighting. While a poll just before the launch of the manifesto had the party at a respectable 7%, in the election the PDs won only 5% of the vote and just four seats. It was lucky to hold that many – at one point it looked as if Liz O'Donnell in Dublin South would be the only survivor.

However, fortune was to smile on the party. Fianna Fáil won 77 seats in that 1997 election, so the FF/PD coalition had just enough seats to form a government with the support of Independents. Out of government with just four TDs, the future would have been bleak for the party. Instead, the PDs were in power just as the country was heading into its biggest ever economic boom. While the party would never again get close to an 11% poll rating (4-5% became its normal range), it did succeed in doubling its seat numbers in the 2002 general election, ensuring the PDs were returned to office as part of the coalition for another five years.

Oh My Darling Clementine

Peter Brooke

THE BACKGROUND

In 1989, Peter Brooke was appointed Secretary of State for Northern Ireland, commonly regarded as the most challenging and difficult position in the British cabinet. He was one of the few ministers to hold onto his position when John Major took over from Margaret Thatcher as leader of the Tory Party in 1990. Affable and thoughtful, Brooke was better regarded than his predecessors in the role.

In 1990, he made the famous statement that the 'British government has no selfish, strategic or economic interest in Northern Ireland', which became the cornerstone of the peace process, opening the way that would lead eventually to the paramilitary ceasefires. However, in 1992, the possibility of peace in Northern Ireland seemed a long way off to most observers. On 17 January, eight Protestant workers were killed by an IRA bomb in a minibus at Teebane, Co Tyrone.

THE GAFFE

That night, Brooke appeared on the *Late Late Show*. He expressed outrage at the attack and sympathy for the victims' families. However, while he declined a request to sing *Danny Boy*, Brooke eventually consented to sing *Oh My Darling Clementine* after much coaxing from host Gay Byrne.

THE IMPACT

There was outrage towards Brooke in the North. Unionists slammed his decision to sing as deeply insensitive and highly inappropriate, given that eight people had been murdered that very day. Although Northern Ireland Office officials argued that to change his itinerary that Friday would have allowed the IRA to set the agenda, there were immediate calls for his resignation. DUP leader Ian Paisley said confidence in Brooke had been 'irretrievably damaged' and the minister had, in effect, 'danced on the graves' of the IRA's victims.

A hugely contrite Brooke addressed the House of Commons in London the following week to report on the attack in Tyrone. He went on to make a direct reference to his appearance on the *Late Late Show*. 'I wish to add a personal word on a subject related to recent events, in which I played a personal role. The decision to maintain the acceptance of a long-standing invitation to go on Mr. Byrne's show in Dublin on Friday night was prompted by the opportunity that it afforded to speak to the people of the Republic of Ireland about terrorism and the

response of a democratic society. Yielding to an unsignalled invitation to sing on the show was innocent in intent, for reasons which are personal to myself, but it was patently an error. Through you, Mr. Speaker, I wish to apologise unreservedly to the families involved in Friday's bombing, to those who represent them in this House and to all those in our wider society who would have taken wholly justified offence.'

Brooke went on to say: 'My commitment to Northern Ireland and its people is, I think, familiar to the House. It is because of that commitment and my understanding of the values and decent opinions of the Province that I have placed my resignation at the Prime Minister's disposal. I also advised him that if he were not to accept it on the spot he should defer any decision on it until after he had concluded his coincidental visit to the Province [Northern Ireland] today.'

Major refused to accept the offer of resignation, describing Brooke as a 'very good friend of peace in Northern Ireland,' and adding: 'He has more work to do yet'. The Northern Secretary also attracted considerable cross party sympathy and support in Westminster. Labour's Northern Ireland spokesman Kevin McNamara praised Brooke's 'characteristically honest and courageous statement' and said he did not see it as a resigning matter. However, there was immediate speculation that the controversy would undermine efforts to start political talks on the future of the North and the view was that Brooke wouldn't survive in the job beyond the pending general election.

He didn't. He was replaced by Patrick Mayhew after Major surprisingly retained power in the general election in April 1992. Brooke did make a brief comeback from the back benches to become Secretary of State for National Heritage until 1994. He stepped down as an MP at the 2001 general election. Instead of being remembered for his historic statement about Britain's lack of 'selfish, strategic or economic interest' in the North, Brooke will always be identified, in Ireland at least, with his unfortunate decision to sing *Oh My Darling Clementine* on the *Late Late Show.*

65

Verbal Delights
Bertie Ahern

THE BACKGROUND

In 1997, Bertie Ahern fulfilled his dream of becoming Taoiseach. In fact, he became the second longest-serving occupant of the office, after Eamon de Valera. He defied those who parodied his penchant for wearing anoraks to develop into a genuine statesman. Ahern's personable and approachable manner have gone down a treat with the voters and he has become the most popular politician since Jack Lynch (who, remember, was described as the most popular politician since Daniel O'Connell).

Although clearly intelligent – Charlie Haughey famously described him as 'the most ruthless, the most devious, the most cunning of them all' – Ahern has never been a great speaker and has become famous for his malapropisms and a somewhat turbulent relationship with the English language.

THE GAFFE

Ahern's verbal slippages have become the stuff of legend. He once told a Fianna Fáil parliamentary party that he wouldn't tolerate anyone forming 'kebabs' within the party (he meant cabals . . . we think).

During a Dáil debate, he continually referred to the Middle East 'road map for peace' as the 'road crash for peace' – many long-time observers of Middle Eastern politics might feel the latter term is more accurate.

Ahern also spoke about not upsetting 'the apple tart' and expressed the view that nobody was going to be hanged 'on the guillotine'. He has described Dublin's Temple Bar as 'Dublin's West Bank' and cautioned people about 'throwing white elephants and red herrings at each other'.

With hindsight, the Taoiseach said, 'we all have 50-50 vision' and he once told the Dáil that he would never condemn wrong-doing (quickly correcting it to 'condone' following prompting from Tanaiste Mary Harney). Cynics may point to the past, but according to Bertie, we live in the future.

Despite a decade in the top job, Ahern's *cúpla focail* have never been of de Valera quality. He once responded to Trevor Sargent in the Dáil with a line straight from the 'Tá sé mahogany gas pipes' school of Irish language. 'Níl me muinteoir', he told the Green Party leader, although the official Dáil record diplomatically records it as 'Níl mé i mo mhuinteoir'.

The gaffes are not confined to the spoken word either. When the Taoiseach signed a book of condolences for the late George Best at the headquarters of the FAI, he expressed 'sympaty' from the 'goverment'. Ironically both words were written exactly as the Taoiseach might actually pronounce them in his distinctive Dublin accent.

THE IMPACT

The gaffes have not remotely damaged Ahern's popularity, arguably having the opposite effect of endearing people to the Taoiseach and adding to his 'man of the people' image. When Bertie boobed with his spelling in signing the George Best book of condolences, 80 percent of listeners who contacted the Ray D'Arcy show on Today FM, during the show's first hour, said this was fine. An hour later, support for him had dropped a bit – the split was 50-50. However, as Bertie Ahern would no doubt observe, still comfortably enough support to win an overall majority.

One listener from Sligo texted in to Today FM to say: 'Leave Bertie alone. At least he can speak his native language unlike a lot of Irish people'. The Sligo listener obviously hadn't heard the 'Níl me muinteoir' line.

Smoke with Fire

John Deasy

THE BACKGROUND

On 29 March, 2004, a ban on smoking was implemented in the workplace by the government with all party support in the Dáil. The radical measure, virtually unprecedented in Europe, meant that smoking was forbidden in workplaces, bars and restaurants.

THE GAFFE

The night after the smoking ban was introduced, Fine Gael's Justice spokesman John Deasy smoked up to three cigarettes in the Oireachtas Members' Bar after being refused access to a small outdoor yard area to smoke. He thus breached the new ban on smoking in the workplace.

THE IMPACT

The smoking ban had captured the imagination of the international media and there had been many predictions in Ireland of widespread non-compliance. While these fears proved groundless, a legislator – particularly a Justice spokesman for the main opposition party – breaching the ban was always going to be big news. The following day, the incident was brought to the attention of the Oireachtas Joint Services Committee of Leinster House.

Fine Gael moved quickly to limit the fallout. Deasy, who already had a testy relationship with Fine Gael leader Enda Kenny before the incident, was fired from the front bench. Kenny stated: 'My business is enforcing standards in the Fine Gael party. Any member of the party who does not live up to those standards will have to live up to the consequences.' Kenny said he sacked Deasy because 'I believe that to restore public confidence in politics then politicians must lead by example. They must behave responsibly and take responsibility for their actions. In this particular instance, I found John Deasy's position as spokesman on Justice to be untenable and I acted accordingly.' He added, 'the law of the land applies here'.

It also emerged that the South Western Area Health Board was investigating the incident in the Dáil bar after the Office of Tobacco Control (OTC) – charged with enforcing the smoking ban – referred the matter to it. The OTC said at the time that it was up to the board's law agent to decide whether to initiate a prosecution. Persons convicted for breaching the ban faced fines of up to €3,000 or three months imprisonment, or both. Ultimately, no prosecution was made.

Despite facing a €3,000 fine, Deasy adopted a *je ne regrette rien* attitude in the days after the incident, attacking the ban as 'extreme'. He expressed frustration that Fine Gael TDs were never given a genuine opportunity to oppose the smoking legislation during its passage through the Dáil. 'I broke the law and I will pay the fine. People might be obeying the law, but they don't like it. The media and politicians have completely lost it. They are not in touch with the people. But I get annoyed when I think that I could be penalised for this when you think of some of the criminal excess that has taken place in the Dáil over the last twenty years,' he told *The Irish Times*. He said he believed the ban was a 'good thing in the long-term' for the country, but even non-smokers believed 'some accommodation' could have been found.

Deasy explained that he had tried to gain access to a yard through a fire-door but bar staff had refused to open it because they did not have permission from the Dáil authorities to do so. 'I tried to comply with the law, but I ended up breaking the law in the end', he said, adding that there was no attempt made to accommodate him and that the law would make 'pariahs of ordinary law-abiding people'. Ironically, the yard was listed by the Dáil authorities as a designated smoking area the day after his actions.

Deasy, who had been elected to the Dáil only two years earlier, admitted that he had become 'fed up' with the Justice portfolio. Intelligent and articulate, Deasy is something of a maverick and a rebel, in the same mould as his father Austin, who had been a government minister. And there was a view in the Dáil that Deasy was happy to be relieved of the restrictions of being on the front bench. The previous year, he had just about survived in the position after disobeying the party whip to vote with the government.

The smoking incident certainly damaged the credibility of the Waterford TD, albeit only in the short term. An editorial in *The Irish Times* said his behaviour was 'contemptuous and arrogant', adding: 'Having formally supported the legislation on behalf of his party as it passed through the Dáil, the example he set for the general public by breaking the law, ignoring the protests of staff in the members' bar and insisting on smoking, could not be tolerated.'

What's Another Year?

John O'Donoghue

THE BACKGROUND

Well-known singer/songwriter Brian Kennedy was chosen to represent Ireland in the 2006 Eurovision Song Contest in an effort to address several years of poor performances by the country in the contest. Kennedy gave a strong rendition of his own composition *Every Song is a Cry for Love* and finished a very respectable 10th in the final, guaranteeing Ireland a place in the following year's final. Finnish monster metal band Lordi won the contest with a stadium-style anthem *Hard Rock Hallelujah*.

THE GAFFE

On the Monday after the final, a press statement appeared on the website of the Department of Arts, Culture and Tourism congratulating Kennedy on his stunning victory. The statement from John O'Donoghue, Minister for the Arts, praised Kennedy on his 'excellent achievement' in bringing Ireland's record

number of Eurovision wins to eight. 'I wish to extend my congratulations to Brian on his marvellous win for Ireland at the Eurovision Song Contest in Athens tonight. He gave a wonderful performance and, in the process, extended Ireland's record number of Eurovision wins to eight,' the statement said. He urged the nation to share in his excitement. 'Everyone should be very proud of this excellent achievement.'

THE IMPACT

Let's face it, the mistake was never going to bring down the government but it did cause much tee-heeing up and down the nation. The statement was posted on the Department's website at 2.30pm and was removed just a half-hour later after listeners to the radio station NewsTalk 106 rang the Sean Moncrieff programme to highlight the error. A spokesman for the Department said: 'This is just a case of human error. The release was drawn up on Saturday [before the contest was held] because we really did think we had a good chance of winning'.

Fine Gael was quick to exploit the minor embarrassment by awarding O'Donoghue – who had been in Cardiff over the weekend watching Munster finally win the European Cup in rugby – 'nul points' (ho, ho!) for the gaffe. The party's Meath TD, Damien English, said: 'If Brian Kennedy's song was a cry for love then it certainly worked on Minister O'Donoghue having moved him so much that he awarded Ireland a record win. It seems there are all kinds of everything that the Minister doesn't know so perhaps he should also note that Biarritz lost the rugby, West Ham lost the FA Cup Final, Arsenal lost the European Cup Final and Dublin lost the hurling'.

Not So Kosher

John Bruton

THE BACKGROUND

April 1995 marked the 50th anniversary of the liberation of the Bergen-Belsen concentration camp in Lower Saxony where tens of thousands of Jews died in horrendous circumstances, including Anne Frank and her sister Margot. To formally mark the occasion, Taoiseach John Bruton sent out invitations to a special ceremony at the War Memorial in Islandbridge, Dublin, followed by a reception in the Royal Hospital, Kilmainham on Saturday, 15 April.

THE GAFFE

Unfortunately for the well-meaning Taoiseach, the date of 15 April was the first day of the Jewish Passover and also the Jewish Sabbath. Eight days before the ceremony was due to take place, *The Irish Times* pointed out the significance of the date to the Taoiseach's office. Two hours later, a spokesman for the Taoiseach said that Bruton would change the date of the commemoration because of the sensitivities of the Jewish community.

THE IMPACT

The Jewish community in Ireland officially commemorated the liberation of Bergen-Belsen with a ceremony in the Terenure synagogue on 26 April rather than on the actual anniversary because of what *The Irish Times* described as 'religious, dietary and other regulations governing the eight-day passover'. After being contacted by the newspaper regarding the change of date, the Taoiseach's spokesman said: 'This sensitivity has been drawn to the Taoiseach's attention and, as a result, he has changed it. He will be consulting with the Jewish community. He will be attending the official ceremony on 26 April.'

The Irish Times said that Bruton might have consulted with Labour TD and Minister for Equality and Law Reform Mervyn Taylor – who is Jewish – on the matter the previous afternoon as he was advised by 'one senior member of the Jewish community' that he could pick a better date.

Alan Shatter, the only Jewish TD ever to be elected for Fine Gael, was asked to comment on what was described in the newspaper as the 'apparent lapse of protocol'. He said he welcomed the fact that a ceremony was being held to commemorate those who lost their lives during the Second World War, especially those victims of the Holocaust. Curiously, given that he was a government TD, the first he had heard of the ceremony was when he received the invitation. He was surprised that the ceremony was being held on the first day of the Jewish Passover and on the Jewish Sabbath, he said, 'because some members of the Jewish community invited in these circumstances may not be able to attend'.

The TD told *The Irish Times* there were strict religious rules as to the type of food members could eat during the Passover and these would pose considerable difficulties in relation to the proposed reception afterwards in the Royal Hospital. 'I'm sure that these difficulties must not have been considered by the Taoiseach or his advisers,' Shatter said. Evidently not. Shatter added pointedly that he was disappointed that the Taoiseach did not contact him beforehand and 'this embarrassment could have been avoided'. A logical enough point, one would have thought, although to be fair to Bruton, his heart was definitely in the right place.

What's in a Name?
Bertie Ahern

THE BACKGROUND

In the 2004 local and European elections, Fianna Fáil took a serious hammering, despite overseeing seven years of prosperity since it came into government. While opinion polls had shown support for the government slipping since its re-election two years earlier, the result still came as a shock to Fianna Fáil and Bertie Ahern. The haemorrhaging of government seats and the resurgence of a Fine Gael party many had thought to be in terminal decline was such that the warning signals could not be ignored. Ahern moved to address the situation.

Finance Minister 'Champagne' Charlie McCreevy was dispatched to Brussels as the government sought to present a more caring, sharing, touchy-feely image to the electorate. Bertie Ahern declared he was a socialist – which, if true, put him alongside Castro and Kim Jong-Il as the only socialist leaders left in the world. And in a move rich with symbolism, McCreevy's nemesis, Fr Sean Healy of CORI (Conference of

Religious in Ireland), was invited to address the parliamentary party in Inchydoney – a gathering that will be forever associated with Ahern's decision to shift his government leftwards.

A year later, the annual think-tank had moved to the Slieve Russell Hotel, Ballyconnell and this time the keynote speaker was Harvard University Professor Robert Putnam, author of the book *Bowling Alone*, which documented social alienation in the US. Putnam's message about the importance of revitalising communities and increasing 'social activisim' was enthusiastically embraced by Ahern, who said he had read *Bowling Alone* a number of times, along with other Putnam books.

Ahern declared that Putnam, whom he described as 'an extraordinary genius', had a major influence on government social policy over the previous decade. Ahern told *The Irish Times*, he had regular contact with Putnam. 'He is a fascinating guy. He was a big adviser of Clinton, who has huge, huge regard for him. He continued on that road with Bush and Blair as well. I'm glad to say we were in talking to him before either of them, since the early 1990s,' said Ahern.

THE GAFFE

In April 2005, in a speech on the future of the community and voluntary sector, the Taoiseach told the audience that 'in his important work on social capital, David Putnam [sic] has traced the processes by which the health of societies can be enhanced or diminished, depending on the extent to which individuals participate in, and feel part of, a wider social reality'. Despite his enthusiasm for Robert Putnam's work and having known him since the early 1990s, Ahern's speech had suggested that David Puttnam – the well-known producer of a host of hit movies including *Chariots of Fire* – rather than Robert Putnam – could help provide the solutions for Ireland's problems in this area. The error was in the script provided to the Taoiseach, rather than being a slip of the tongue .

THE IMPACT

Unfortunately for the Taoiseach, although the speech was not widely covered at the time, the error ultimately surfaced on the radar screen of Senan Moloney, political correspondent for the *Irish Independent*. In an article written after the speech was given, the *Irish Independent* revealed that government officials had moved to cover up 'Bertie Ahern's latest gaffe' and that the speech had 'mysteriously disappeared from government websites'. Despite their efforts, it remains possible to access both versions on the internet – one paying tribute to Robert Putnam, the other crediting David Puttnam.

David Robert Putnam, we'll never forget you.

The Celtic Snail

Fine Gael

THE BACKGROUND

Coming towards the end of 2000, Fine Gael was in trouble. A general election loomed on the horizon. Despite the various controversies that the Fianna Fáil/Progressive Democrats government had been involved in – including the O'Flaherty affair (see Chapter 24) which should have proved devastating for the coalition – the main opposition party was struggling badly in the opinion polls.

Leader John Bruton's personal popularity rating was the lowest of the main party leaders. Fine Gael was internally divided. Many heavy hitters such as Michael Noonan, Jim Mitchell and Alan Dukes felt left out of the decision-making process, which was dominated – they believed – by Bruton and a small number of people around him, including his brother Richard, deputy leader Nora Owen, Phil Hogan and the party's general secretary Tom Curran.

THE GAFFE

With the Celtic Tiger at its peak, there was clearly no political mileage in tackling the government on economic performance. Instead Fine Gael decided to build on a perception that voters were frustrated about quality of life issues and by the contrast between a dynamic economy and the slow pace in delivering solutions to problems such as traffic congestion, hospital waiting lists and high costs of childcare. The result in November 2000 was the 'Celtic Snail' poster (featuring the eponymous creature) and a press campaign at an estimated cost of IR£160,000. The campaign, which was put together by the agency DDFH&B, included 350 posters placed nationwide.

Explaining the campaign, Fine Gael said: 'There's something in the way we do things in Ireland which seems to clog up progress towards a better quality of life. Heeldragging. Procrastination. Dithering. Vested interests. We call it the Celtic Snail. In this era of the Celtic Tiger, progress on so many issues is painfully slow. What is stalling the creation of adequate and affordable childcare? How long must our hospitals be underequipped and understaffed? Why is a proper transport system for Dublin taking so long? What, if anything, is being done for the victims of crime? When are the aged going to be treated with the respect they deserve? In Fine Gael we believe we have identified the outdated conventions that are blocking social progress and better infrastructure in this country. We believe we can remove the blockages and obstacles to getting things right. And we are committed to tackling them. It's time to speed things up. Time to eradicate the Celtic Snail. Fine Gael's Plan for the Nation sets out the way.'

THE IMPACT

The campaign was an unmitigated disaster, which was widely ridiculed and provided the catalyst for a successful leadership challenge to Bruton by Michael Noonan.

Even with hindsight, it's difficult to come up with solid reasons as to why the posters flopped so badly. Many of the points made by Fine Gael were virtually beyond dispute. However, perception is everything in politics and the perception then, and now, was that the Celtic Snail campaign stunk.

Advertising experts had their own views on why it failed to make an impact. 'From an advertising viewpoint the consumer issue is very valid, but, unfortunately, it was badly executed,' one senior executive said shortly after the launch. Noting that the poster was a pun on the Celtic Tiger, he said puns are always pedestrian and lazy. 'There are so many vehicles for politicians to get their message across. Why waste the money on this?' he asked.

Another advertising executive said the problem with using a negative image was 'you tend to get lumbered with it. The fact that snail rhymed with Fine Gael was unfortunate and should have been spotted.'

He also suggested that the idea was too complicated for a 48-sheet poster. 'If you were travelling at 30 or 40 miles an hour there's no possibility you would have remotely understood it.'

'It may have seemed like the perfect analogy: a snail is slow and slimy and Fine Gael wanted to suggest that the government was slow to capitalise on the economic boom and that the tribunals had tarnished Fianna Fáil's image. But Fine Gael has hardly been a shining example of how an opposition party should conduct itself,' said another top advertising executive.

However, to be fair to the people who developed the concept, the reasons for its failure may have had less to do with the actual campaign and more to do with a major credibility problem that Fine Gael had with the electorate at the time.

Bruton's leadership was living on borrowed time. While he had comfortably survived a no-confidence motion in November 2000, the widespread criticism of the Celtic Snail campaign further demoralised an already deflated party. In January 2000, the combined forces of Noonan and Jim Mitchell – buoyed by his success in chairing the DIRT inquiry – launched a challenge. Mitchell cited the Celtic Snail campaign as a classic example of Bruton's centralised style of leadership. 'The front bench never discussed the Celtic Snail. We were told about it on the day it was being launched . . . and that's a classic case of what happens frequently.'

Noonan and Mitchell won the day and Bruton's leadership was over. While a second phase of the Celtic Snail campaign had been planned for the Fine Gael Ard Fheis in the spring, it never materialised. The snail was left sitting in his shell. Gone, but not forgotten.

Barrington's: PD or not PD?

Des O'Malley

THE BACKGROUND

Just before Christmas 1985, a new political party was established by former Fianna Fáil minister Des O'Malley with the aim of breaking the mould of Irish politics. His new party, the Progressive Democrats, promised to cut taxes, curb public spending and generally bring a more responsible and ethical approach to Irish politics. Their message was enthusiastically received by the electorate. In the 1987 general election, the party won 14 seats and almost 12% of the vote. That election saw a minority Fianna Fáil government elected.

Charlie Haughey surprised everybody by doing a u-turn on Fianna Fáil election promises and set about taking the tough decisions needed to address the mess in the country's public finances. Furthermore, Fine Gael's leader, Alan Dukes, announced that he would support the government as long as it adhered to strict control of the public finances. Dukes' strategy of support became known as the Tallaght Strategy. Despite their electoral success, the PDs were in a difficult position – acting as a critical opposition party, while the government, backed by Fine Gael, adopted a similar economic strategy to the one the PDs had first advocated.

THE GAFFE

The Minister for Health, Rory O'Hanlon, announced the closure of the outdated Barrington's Hospital in Limerick as part of a series of cutbacks designed to restore order to the public finances. There was an angry reaction in Limerick to the decision and O'Malley, a TD for the city, firmly backed the local cause. He took part in a protest march and in the Dáil the PDs put down a private member's motion against the closure.

THE IMPACT

It was a PR disaster for the PDs and seriously damaged the party's credibility. It had presented itself as the party of fiscal rectitude, yet when it came to the leader's own constituency, it seemed as if the PDs were not prepared to practice what they preached. Of course, it was a difficult issue for the PDs, particularly given the local emphasis of Irish politics. But the PDs were supposed to be different. In the eyes of their critics, they had talked the talk for almost two years but when it came to crunch time, they had notably failed to walk the walk.

Defending his position during the private member's motion in February 1988, O'Malley argued, 'there is an assumption on the

part of some media commentators and also some members of the public that if one believes in the control of public expenditure and the reduction of the appalling deficits and debt which we have, then one must necessarily support every move and every proposal made in a financial context by this Government, irrespective of how demonstrably foolish the particular proposal may be and irrespective of the existence of more sensible alternatives.'

He added that he did not 'subscribe to this blank cheque approach which takes from the Government the onus to get things right . . . The Government take the view that in Limerick one hospital is as good as another and that it is largely the toss of a coin which should decide if one hospital has to be closed. . . They are closing down a hospital which, apart from the orthopaedic hospital in Croom, has the two most modern operating theatres in the mid-west and which has extensive X-ray facilities for a substantial accident and emergency service. They are closing a hospital which, on the Department of Health's figures, is far more cost efficient per occupied bed than any other hospital in Limerick.' He claimed that 'of all unwise decisions that have been made, this one must surely be the craziest of all. The Minister for Health is closing a hospital that contains the facilities that the taxpayer will have to provide in another hospital 500 or 600 yards away which does not have those facilities.'

The response from Minister Rory O'Hanlon was cutting: 'This issue has been a good acid test for the Progressive Democratic Party. Where now are the statements of principle and the clarion calls for cutbacks? Where now is the much vaunted ideology of free enterprise? Where now are the mould breakers of Irish politics? . . . When these Deputies have to face a point of principle on their front doors as they do today, their courage evaporates, their principles disintegrate and their images crumble. I think, perhaps, that on this occasion, they have forsaken national politics for parochial party politics. Here we have a party without direction. The reasons they thought they had for existence are no more'.

While O'Malley might have had a point about whether or not the right hospital was being closed, there was unease within his own party at the stance. Quoted in Stephen Collins' definitive book on the party, *Breaking the Mould – How the PDs Changed Irish Politics*, Mary Harney said she was 'totally against' the party's stance on Barrington's. 'We have never recovered from it. Here was an issue in Des O'Malley's backyard and the party adopted a position that did not fit with its overall policy. Des' position was that a hospital in Limerick should close, but it should be St John's, not Barrington's. That message was impossible to get across and the issue was a huge disaster for us.'

Former press secretary of the PDs Stephen O'Byrnes also regarded it as a low point in the party's history. He told Stephen Collins: 'Barrington's Hospital did enormous damage. Here we were, the party of fiscal rectitude, not being prepared to follow the prescription in the leader's own constituency. In my view, it was fundamental as it represented a failure of the party to live up to one of its fundamental principles.'

It's a moot point as to whether the issue damaged the party in the long term. In the general election 16 months later in 1989, the party lost eight seats, but that can't be explained by any one factor. After that election, the PDs entered government with Fianna Fáil. Except for one spell of four and a half years on the opposition benches, it has been there ever since.

Irish Family Feuds

Battles over Money, Sex and Power

LIAM COLLINS

When families fall out, the bitterness that emerges is matched only by the ferocity of their attacks on each other. Family feuds are far more vicious than disputes between strangers, as family members compete to crush each other completely and without mercy.

Cases include many rich and famous Irish families:

- Ben v Margaret – Duel at Dunnes
- the PV Doyle family 'hotel' war
- Comans and the 'Pub brawl'
- Enya, Clannad and the Brennan family feud
- 'Volkswagon vendetta' – the O'Flahertys' family secret

and many more family feuds over money, power and sex.

Great GAA Moments 2006

FINBARR McCARTHY

Foreword by GAA President, Nickey Brennan

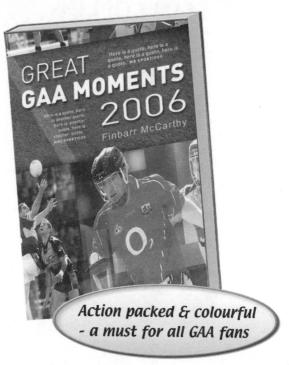

Action packed & colourful - a must for all GAA fans

From the drama of the Omagh Brawl to jubilant celebrations of the 'West's Awake', as both Club Championship titles travelled back across the Shannon; from the tension created by the GPA's threat to strike, to the clash of the best hurling and football teams on this island, the year was packed with unforgettable GAA events.

Covers the All-Ireland Football and Hurling Finals, DJ Carey's Retirement, Managerial Casualties, and much more.

Accompanied by superb action shots from the field, *Great GAA Moments 2006* brings to the reader images and tales of a spectacular season in Gaelic sport.

Erindipity

<u>The</u> Irish Miscellany

DAVID KENNY

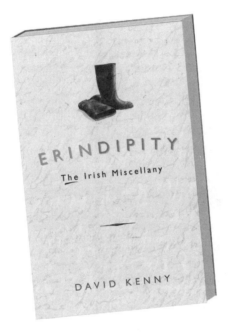

Erindipity – the ultimate Irish miscellany – is like that Irish stew your mad granny used to make after she'd cleared out the back of the cupboard. Each time you dip your spoon in, out comes something unexpected!

Ever wondered how many teeth Richard Harris lost to get nominated for an Oscar? Do you know long it takes to pluck a turkey in Cavan – or re-feather a chicken in Dalkey? Or how about: the nearest entrance to Hell, the biggest wellie race, the smelliest place, the best thing to do with a corpseless head, or the largest amount of ice cream ever lost at sea?

The book also includes the following subjects – and much more!